TRAFFIC DATA COLLECTION

(Proceedings of the conference held at the Institution of
Civil Engineers, 5-6 April 1978)

Institution of Civil Engineers

London, 1978

A joint conference between the Department of Transport,
the Institution of Electrical Engineers, and
the Institution of Civil Engineers.

Organizing Committee:

M.G. Cooke (Chairman)
I.M. Dow
P.L. Belcher

Production Editor:

Anthony M. Burt

© The Institution of Civil Engineers, 1978

ISBN   0 7277 0070 7

Published by the Institution of Civil Engineers.
Distributed by Thomas Telford Ltd for
the Institution of Civil Engineers, Telford House,
PO Box 101, 26-34 Old Street, London EC1P 1JH.

Contents

Opening address

THE CHAIRMAN: Mr R.J. Bridle, BSc
Department of Transport

The purpose of the Road Board in organizing this conference
stems from several concerns. Chief amongst them has been
the suspicions engineers have expressed about the quality of
the traffic data collected and the sensitivity of its interpretation. The Department of Transport and local authorities are certainly troubled about its cost-effectiveness and
the lack of credibility expressed by the public about decisions based on the data. Then it is also true that the
industry involved in providing equipment for traffic observation has expressed doubts about customer needs and the way
in which research and development has been conducted. They
have suggested greater involvement on their part.

If we, in the Department of Transport were a firm supply-
ing customers, in this instance the people using highways
and it was my responsibility to advise the managing director
on the effectiveness of the market research and on the
extent to which it maximized return and reduced uncertainty,
my Protestant ethic background would cause me to blush
furiously. My conscience would prick me because I believe
that market research in this diverse field could stand a
great deal of improvement.

The Road Board recognized that over the last few years a
number of initiatives have been taken, but in separate areas.
There have been initiatives with the Electrical Industry
Traffic Aids Committee (EITAC) the structure by which the
Department consults with the Electrical Industries, there
have been the considerable departmental initiative through
the Regional Highway Traffic Model (RHTM) and Local Authorities have joined with the Department in forming the regional
Standing Traffic Data Liaison Committees (STDLCs). However,
the Road Board was concious that the interface between those
concerned with the equipment and those concerned with speci-
fying the data to be collected was not being bridged and no

1

forum for discussion of this interface existed. The Road
Board therefore believed that there was a considerable need
for a conference of this kind.

   In discussion, the Road Board developed fourteen questions
which it considered needed to be answered by the conference.
Some are perfunctory, others are contentions but all need
answers.

(a) What is collected and how?
(b) What is the data used for?
(c) What could the data be used for?
(d) What other data would be useful?
(e) What are the current inaccuracies?
(f) What are their causes?
(g) What is the need for their removal?
(h) How sensitive to the accuracy of the data are the
     decisions made upon them?
(i) What is the cost of removing the inaccuracies?
(j) What is the range of the methods of collection and
     their cost trends?
(k) What are the problems of administering processing and
     retrieving the data?
(l) What risks are involved in changing to a new system.
(m) What frameworks are necessary to answer the questions
     and who should be involved?
(n) What decisions are recommended?

With question (a) it is true that a clear statement is necessary and the early papers set out to do this while Paper 6
deals exclusively with (e) to (g). The cost of removing
inaccuracies will no doubt take up part of the discussion.

   The Road Board considered (j) important as it believes there
was some room for lateral thinking. Current improvements
appeared to be increments along a fixed line of development.
The cost trend of manual collection was increasing, but the
cost trend of automatic collection was decreasing and this
would have significant implications for new systems. However,
the risks of changeover needed careful consideration since if
everything is changed at once, risks have to be multiplied
together, but if changes are evolutionary, risks are only
additive although there may be other risks involved.

   Finally discussion should not ignore the frameworks necessary to manage a system which covers many authorities' res-
ponsibilities. I do not suppose for one moment that all
these questions will be answered, or even discussed. The
questions cover enough material to keep the Department of
Transport and TRRL busy for quite a few years yet but it is
hoped that the conference will be a notable forum for influencing thinking on the subject .

I. Setting the scene - data uses present and future

R.E. Fry, BSc, MIS
Departments of the Environment and Transport

SYNOPSIS. This paper provides a summary review of traffic
data collection systems and needs at the national level ie
within the Department of Transport. The aim is to present
a framework within which other more detailed contributions
to this conference can be located. It begins with an
exposition of the department's present data collection
arrangements, not in terms of the specific censuses and
surveys, which are to be described in other papers; but
rather in terms of the data needs now being met. This is
followed by a discussion of the way in which over time new
needs for information have emerged in various policy and
highway planning and management areas. The paper concludes
with an outline of the ideas for reform of the system which
are being developed in a departmental Working Group set up
for this purpose.

THE PRESENT TRAFFIC DATA COLLECTION SYSTEMS

1. The department presently controls a variety of regular
traffic censuses and surveys most of which have been
established for some years. Many involve nationally distributed samples of traffic counting sites and are carried
out by local authorities acting as agents of the department.
Almost all of this straight traffic counting is presently
undertaken through the use of human enumerators counting
over short periods and manually recording the data. Until
quite recently only a small amount of such volumetric
traffic counting was undertaken on a continuous basis,
using automatic counters linked to sensors on the road
surface (pneumatic tubes or inductive wire loops). The
regular use of automatic counters has recently increased
for special purposes such as providing input to the
Regional Highway Traffic Models now under development

for traffic forecasting purposes; or for motorway traffic
control development. However such uses are not yet fully
integrated into the department's overall system of traffic
censuses and surveys.

2. For the purposes of this paper, the main system is best
described in terms of its principal underlying aims.
Firstly there is the statistical aim of providing a
numerical description of the traffic characteristics of
the road network (eg vehicle-kilometres by type of vehicle)
important for general policy and research. This is undertaken by the use of large-scale but infrequent 'benchmark'
censuses at intervals of several years, supplemented by
very much smaller surveys on a 'core' of fixed sites,
undertaken several times a year in order to monitor trends
and the seasonal flow variation of different classes of
vehicle.

3. Secondly there is the aim of providing traffic flow
data related to specific road links useful as part of the
input for the design, assessment and management of highway
schemes. This is partly provided by a programme of more
intensive traffic flow measurements, (the General Traffic
Census) undertaken on a very large sample of road links
covering all the main types of road, tackled consecutively
over a period of years.

4. Finally, there is a need for some continuous year-
round traffic flow measurement on various types of road in
order to establish patterns of hourly flow and seasonal
variation. This is necessary in order to calculate factors
for the transformation of the short-period, manually
recorded counts in the main censuses into such quantities
as peak flow, annual average daily flow, etc, required,
inter alia, for the design and assessment of highway
schemes. Over the years, such information has been provided by a small sample of automatic traffic counters.

5. Information other than straight traffic volume measurements has so far been obtained by various ad hoc surveys.
Examples are surveys of vehicle speeds to assess the
effects of speed limits; or the monitoring of before-and-
after vehicle separation distances to determine the effects
of road safety advertising campaigns. Similarly, axle
loadings of commercial vehicles have been monitored at a
number of weighbridge sites in order to provide research
information for road pavement design purposes and to help
provide broad inuications of national axle loading
patterns. And so on.

6. This long-established corpus of regular and ad hoc
censuses and surveys is as important for its various purposes as it ever was and compares very favourably with
similar systems in many other developed countries. However in recent years, changing circumstances have extended
the range of information required and increased the need
for some reform of the system. That reform would cover
firstly improvements in the quality, the structure and the
organisation of the traffic counts which form the heart of
the present system; and secondly the measurement of new
traffic parameters such as speeds, headway between vehicles,
extended vehicle classifications, axle weights etc which
are now needed more frequently and with greater coverage
than previously, as an input to road safety policy, and
highway planning and management generally.

7. It is hardly possible in a short paper of this nature
to discuss effectively the full range of information needs
which can now be identified and which underpin the case
for reform. However the principal regular requirements
have been touched upon in preceding paragraphs. Other
requirements in this general area of traffic studies (by
no means less important) would call for information on
such items as

> Journey data (origins and destinations, journey speeds,
> trip purposes, vehicle occupancies).
>
> Axle spacings.
>
> Junction flows.
>
> Delay measurements.
>
> Weather and visibility observations.
>
> Pedestrian flows.
>
> Road lane occupancies.

It will be apparent that some of these are different in
nature to the measurement of the physical characteristics
of road traffic and perhaps fall outside the scope of this
conference. Further discussion of data needs in this paper
will therefore concern itself with improvements required
in traffic count data and the need for new kinds of
measurements already touched upon in paragraph 6.

IMPROVEMENTS REQUIRED IN TRAFFIC COUNT DATA

8. The range of vehicle types using our roads has
increased over recent years, particularly among freight
vehicles. This phenomenon with its implications for road
safety, road maintenance, environmental effects, road
pavement design, etc has led to an interest in a more
detailed vehicle classification for use in categorising
road traffic counts. Some of these elaborations in
vehicle classification are difficult or impossible to
implement through human enumerators. Automatic counters
as they are now being developed offer the possibility of
registering physical dimensions (length, weight, number
of axles) which permit some of the required extensions of
the classification not otherwise possible, though not all.

9. There is also an urgent need for an improvement in the
standards of accuracy and consistency now associated with
collection of data by visual observation. Such deficiencies
arise from the problems of supervising a large field force
of observers so as to ensure an acceptable and uniform
error rate due to miscounting and misclassification.
Further difficulties arise from the need to restrict such
counting to comparatively short periods for reasons of
cost and practicability. This generates technical problems of deriving estimates of parameters of the total
traffic flow over longer periods. Once again, the continuity and consistency of automatic traffic counters
offer the prospect of a solution. However experience
shows that they bring new problems in the way of equipment
reliability, equipment protection and the editing of data
which has been subjected to interruption or distortion due
to breakdown or unforeseen circumstances. Such problems
are not insoluble although much work remains to be done.

10. Concerning accuracy, it is important to note that
although there is plenty of scope for improvements in the
error rate in the primary count data, even so, the variability due to sampling in time or space, weather conditions, local traffic events (parked vehicles, accidents,
roadworks, temporary traffic management measure, etc) will
inevitably be present whatever measurement technique is
used.

11. Finally there is a need to improve the organisation
and accessibility of the traffic count data. Arrangements
for storing, processing and integrating the output of the
various censuses are by no means adequate or sufficiently
coordinated. For example, there is frequently no simple

way of linking together various data sets relating to the same road section. If there should be in the future a move towards a greater degree of automatic counting, a more efficient way of handling the much greater volumes of data that will ensue, will be a prime consideration.

THE NEEDS FOR NEW KINDS OF MEASUREMENTS

12. Mention has already been made of the fact that parameters such as speed, vehicle spacing, the loading of axles etc have for some time been measured to a limited extent. More recently, there has been a growing demand for these variables to be monitored regularly, for longer periods, on a more widespread basis.

13. Here again, developments in automatic detection equipment seem potentially capable of meeting the technical requirements. Perhaps the main difficulty arises from the fact that there are very large variations in, for example, speed and headway, over the network and over time. Meaningful national statistics of the frequency distribution of such parameters representative of the whole road network would imply the use of comparatively elaborate equipment at a prohibitively large number of sites, with consequentially high capital and maintenance costs. However, it seems rather more feasible to obtain trend indications eg of vehicles exceeding speed limits, by taking regular measurements at a sample of say 30 to 50 sites. This might ideally be reinforced by a system of mobile counters capable of being transferred as required to monitor areas of special interest, although its feasibility remains to be explored.

14. Reference was made in paragraph 11 to the need for better management of the data output of traffic counters. If additionally there is to be a regular, though more limited flow of the other sorts of measurements just discussed and including perhaps even weather observations, highway characteristics etc, then this suggests that all such information should also be capable of being linked through a family of data banks in which the common unit is the road section to which the observations refer. It would be necessary to examine such a concept carefully to ensure that its operational usefulness justified the costs and difficulties of creating and up-dating the data banks.

7

SOME POSSIBLE WAYS FORWARD

15. Since mid-1976, a Departmental Working Group including observers from some other government departments and the Association of County Councils has been reviewing the department's system of traffic censuses and working towards a set of options for their reform. At the time of writing, ideas on the nature of these options are beginning to take shape although no final decisions have been taken, and formal consultation with local authorities has yet to take place.

16. Two main lines of thought have emerged. One is that the broad structure of the present traffic censuses should remain but with some changes to ensure greater economy in the use of road sites, and more efficient statistical estimation through improved sampling of sites and timing of counts. In this, the most important change would be the gradual changeover to the comprehensive use of automatic counters in the smallest (200-point) census which is carried out several times each year in order to establish trends (see paragraph 2). This 'core' census would serve several purposes. It would give improved accuracy and consistency of trend data; it would provide a much wider range of continuous traffic data serving to improve the quality of the factors required to derive from the larger short-period manual censuses such quantities as annual average daily flow; and it would simultaneously provide many of the requirements of the newly developed Regional Highway Traffic Models. Finally it would permit the use of some of the automatic counters for the regular monitoring of new parameters such as speeds, headways and axle loadings.

17. Perhaps the aspect of this first option which has most revealed a conflict of interests is the proposal to confine the census of link-specific data (the General Traffic Census - see paragraph 3) to the motorway and trunk roads for which the department is responsible. In this respect, the second option to emerge from the Working Group is particularly relevant since over the longer term, it would actually widen the range of link-specific data.

18. This is a more radical scheme in which sampling of sites would be based on a computerised register of all links in the road network. The sampling system envisaged is relatively complex and will not be described here in detail but it has the following main characteristics. The register would be stratified by such characteristics as

region, road class, urban/rural, road link length, permitting systematic statistical design of samples of sites for counting. There would be a quarterly cycle of sampling of about 500 points comprising some which would be fixed, some repeating sites from the previous quarter and some fresh sites not covered for at least five years. The arrangement would be designed to produce over time a wide but systematic coverage of the network so that in a 5-year cycle, more than 4,000 points will have been counted at least once. A major part of the counting would be automatic, but a substantial component of manual counting would remain in order (for example) to produce those aspects of vehicle classification with which automatic counters are unable to cope. The system would produce all the main outputs required and foreseen, at the cost of some increased complexity in methods of estimation. Its principal additional advantages lie in the fact that its rotating sampling system is less vulnerable to the gradual changes in the shape and nature of the network than is the present rather rigid sampling structure; and in the fact that it can produce a wide range of link-specific data covering all types of road both classified and unclassified.

19. The practical difference between the two schemes lies in the fact that the first would be relatively easy to move towards from the present position, whereas the second involves comparatively drastic changes difficult to achieve in their entirety except over a long period. Both have found substantial support among the various interests. It seems possible that some attempt may be made to achieve short-term useful reform by moving initially in the direction of the first option, while planning changes and work using the RHTM road link data bank as the nucleus, to permit movement over time towards the greater flexibility and more comprehensive structure of the second scheme.

2. Setting the scene - present methods of collection and analysis - an International comparison of data collection means

G.A.C. Searle, MBA, MSc
Department of Transport

SYNOPSIS. To serve as a reference source for the
Conference, details are given of the Department of
Transport's current, regular framework for collecting
traffic flow data. The collection of other traffic data,
for instance including parameters other than flow such as
axle load, is then touched upon. This is followed by a
brief summary of the apparent state of the art in a number
of other West European countries. A comment is then made
about uses, needs and requirements. The paper concludes
with some personal views on the inherent limitations of
traffic data and its collection, limitations that expose as
impractical any counsel of perfection in this field.

INTRODUCTION

1. I want to do several things in the 20 minutes available
to me. These include aspects of traffic data which it has
fallen to my lot to present to you in this early talk, to
provide a better foundation for our discussions; on these
I can claim no special expertise in relation to others
present, nor any major responsibility, favourable or un-
favourable, for our present state of affairs. But then
having done my duty to you all in this more institutional
role, I would like the privilege for 5 minutes or so to
become more myself, as it were, and give you some more
personal views on some of the more fundamental difficulties
t o which I think we should be alert.

2. So to start with I shall outline to you the present
system of traffic data collection in this country. I shall
then make a passing reference to what we know of the methods
currently in use in one or two other countries whose
practice should be of interest to us. I then want to make

a first shot - I am sure that more will be said on this
subject later in the Conference - on uses, needs and
requirements for traffic data. Finally, I shall be more
myself and tell you why I think we would be silly to try
to do and expect too much of any traffic data system.

The Present System

3. The prime framework for traffic data collection is the
Department of Transport's (please translate appropriately
for Scotland and Wales); but this does not mean of course
that the Department's role in this field is, or can be,
absolute. This framework consists of the various, fairly
well-known, series of censuses as follows:

i. General Traffic Census: this is a manual,
classified census i.e. the data is recorded
manually and classified into various vehicle classes,
in this case motorcycles, cars, light vans, buses
and coaches, several sub-classes of heavier goods
vehicle (2-axled, 3-axled rigid, 4-axled rigid, 3-
axled articulated, and finally 4 or more axled
articulated) and optionally pedal cycles or cars
with trailers. The GTC covers Motorways, Trunk Roads
and Principal Roads, the actual points which are
representative of road links being spread about on a
rough sampling basis. The GTC is "annual", with
6,250 points in all rotated so that each point is
counted once every 4 or 5 years. The count is
primarily an August one, but a $\frac{1}{4}$ of all points are
recounted as a seasonal check in the following April
or May. GTC counts are, strictly, always for both
a Sunday and Monday, for 16 hours.

ii. The 200-point census, which is also a manual
classified one. The vehicle classes here are similar
to those in the GTC, except that pedal cycles are
always counted and mopeds and scooters are counted
separately from motor cycles proper. The essential
point about the 200-point census is that it is
monthly, and carried out on a strictly random sample
of sites: the prime use of this census is for
estimating national vehicle mileage trends, and the
data is also used for estimating the national
seasonal variation of flows for the various vehicle
classes.

iii. 50-point automatic census: this census is currently
operated by the TRRL, and employs loops and tubes

for the automatic traffic counting. This is the only
continuous national census. The points are (very)
fixed, although they were randomly selected. It is
this census that is the standard source of data on
traffic flow disaggregated in terms of hours, days,
weeks and months throughout the year; it is also
used to provide an independent check on overall
vehicle mileage levels.

iv. 1,300-point (benchmark) manual classified census.
The vehicle classes here are the same as for the 200-
point census. This census is run about once every 6
years, at a random sample of sites representative of
the whole road network, and the 200-point census sites
(which are only on classified roads) form a subset of
it. Its main purpose is to provide "benchmark"
estimates of vehicle mileages by vehicle class, region
and road type (including unclassified roads). The 200-
point census, which is modified as necessary according
to the benchmark results, is then used to up-date
these figures to provide the regular estimates of
traffic trends.

At this point, I should emphasise that this is the current
framework that we have, as it has grown up over the years.
This framework is purely addressed to the problem of
counting traffic flows (with consequent estimation of
vehicle mileage) at specified points in time and space, on
some sample basis. This is not of course the only traffic
counting that is done. The Department does a considerable
amount of additional traffic counting, largely on an ad hoc
basis, where more data is needed in relation to a particular
road scheme, for instance. Similarly, a large amount of
data is also collected by local authorities. The framework
identified above has been fixed for some years now; in fact,
the basic concept and parts of it are old indeed. Changes
are in prospect: Mr Fry chairs a Working Group which is
looking into the whole question, and hopefully some
decisions, perhaps for a major re-orientation in the long
term, will be taken fairly early in 1978. We also have the
Regional Highway Traffic Model and the Standing Traffic
Data Liaison Committees (STDLC's) which offer the prospect
of an improved integration of national traffic data for the
future; for RHTM a sample of automatic network monitoring
sites has been established, the prime aim of which is to
relate short period flows on any section of the RHTM network to the corresponding flows on a different time basis
(e.g. for a whole year).

4. There is a great deal of other information collected
which is also sensibly regarded as traffic data. For
instance, all accident data is initially recorded by the
police on the Stats 19 form (a recent revision of form is
to be introduced by some police forces in January 1978), and
this is coded and stored in a computer. Lorries are
weighed in terms of their axle loads for various purposes by
various people; this is an important function, because the
damage done to road pavements is a large power of the axle
load. Large amounts of traffic data are also collected for
more background purposes - for instance, traffic speeds in
connection with speed limit policy, and for determining the
basic speed-flow relationships. The forgoing is simply a
small sample of what is done outside the "basic system".
It is virtually impossible to establish anything like a
complete list of such data collection: I would like simply
to put into your minds for the Conference that there are
many traffic data activities and requirements other than
the simple measurement of flows at specified points.

Other Countries

5. I maintain that it is difficult enough finding out
sufficient about what is going on in this country; there
is therefore, for the wary, a need to be cautious about the
practices in other countries. We cannot claim to have what
I would consider to be adequate, authoritative information,
and so in statistical terms I can only present to you a
very rudimentary sketch. Perhaps others attending the
Conference can add to this if appropriate. Nevertheless, I
think that we have a proper "feeling" on the subject, and
that is that nobody is doing the difficult job of traffic
counting marvelously better than ourselves: all countries
obviously face similar difficulties in this field, and
nobody has the "perfect solution".

6. The French Ministry has kindly sent me some of their
current documents for presentation to you in this paper. A
permanent census of traffic on the national network has
existed in France since 1968 for inter-urban roads, and
since 1976 for towns of between 5,000 and 20,000 in-
habitants. This network includes the Routes Nationales and
Autoroutes. The results of this census are grouped by
region and by Department, and published annually. Automatic, permanent traffic counts are made about every 30km,
yielding sometimes daily, sometimes hourly, flows,
according to the traffic level. The system for the non-
tolled sections of Autoroutes is labelled "temporary" (as

opposed to "permanent" for the RN). The message to us from
this is clear: the French have recently instituted a
system of simple automatic counting to obtain traff⌐   ⌐ws
for their Routes Nationales and Autoroutes system;   is
not directly integrated with counting on local roads,
does it provide the means for classifying by vehicle type;
it is equivalent to our own 50-point census, but with a much
larger number of points for the major road network only.

7. We also have some knowledge of Dutch practice, as a
result of a helpful visit there by DTp Statisticians about
a year ago. The Dutch also primarily rely on a system of
permanent automatic traffic counters, of which there are
265 spread throughout the country on rural roads on a
"representative" basis: these give a monthly traffic index.
But the Dutch have also considered a monthly rotating sample
of automatic counters to cover all road sections over a 5
year period; counting is also now done on this basis as
well, but as yet only to obtain <u>annual</u> flows at the
rotated points. Interestingly, the Netherlands has the
problem that road classes are defined differently from one
province to another. Automatic vehicle classification
equipment is currently being installed at some sites, with
development work to measure also the number of axles of
vehicles and to link to dynamic load-weighing equipment.
They have no standard system for collecting vehicle speeds
and headways; nor any standardised system for dis-
aggregating vehicle-kilometres by vehicle class. (There is
other information in a Dutch ECE paper, stating that each
month there is an automatic classification of vehicles at
half the permanent sites into one of three length bands.)

8. The Federal Republic of Germany appears to rely on
manual, short-term counts, extrapolated by means of some
automatic, long-term counts. In 1977, the Germans were
sceptical of the possibility of automatically dis-
tinguishing between more than 2 categories of vehicles
using automatic devices.

<u>Uses, Needs and Requirements</u>

9. It is easy to say: of course we need traffic data, and
much more of it, in order to design and operate the road
system, to make it safer, and so on. I hope that in this
Conference we will not take such a blanket belief as
axiomatic. As I shall argue shortly, I believe that there
are inherent, permanent limitations on the amount and
quality of data we can expect. Moreover, there are obvious
costs: traffic data collection is neither free nor pain-

less, and for economic reasons alone a limit must be
accepted, as it now currently is in relation to the basic
framework of data I described earlier; the resources to
organise the collection of traffic data and to analyse it
are valuable and scarce, not just in principle but in
current reality.

10. As I made clear earlier, I cannot hope to present a
complete shopping list of current uses and needs: let us
stop pretending that this is completely possible. Also I
am sure we would all agree, even my Statistician
colleagues who have the responsibility for compiling data
series, that we are not simply in the game of collecting
data for its own sake. Let me then suggest a thesis.
This is that basically the existing framework satisfies
needs quite well: it provides the basis of forecasts of
future traffic and energy requirements, for instance,
through the analysis of past national trends; and for the
specifics of road planning and scheme design, it does
enable us to make estimates of annual traffic levels and
the like from limited local counts outside the framework.
Thus I have identified important uses and needs of such
data. But the coherence of this framework, the way it fits
together, is now questionable in detail, and it seems
certain that something better could be devised for the same
cost that would improve the basic traffic flow data
available to central and local government. Our ability to
disaggregate the available data in terms of vehicle class,
road type and region is poor at present; and while,
consistent with my general thesis, in many respects this
does not matter, there are some important aspects in which
it is important - for instance the use of more minor roads
by heavy lorries, and the implications for highway
maintenance.

11. That is all I want to say about traffic <u>flow</u> here. In
principle, accident data is well handled through the revised
Stats 19 form, although in the past there have been major
difficulties in breaking out this information, because of
errors in recording, and difficulties in accessing the
stored data (and there is a warning here regarding
aspirations for comprehensive data banks): so at the
moment we do not have a good enough idea of the relative
accident rates of different classes and weights of lorries,
a not unimportant subject; and our minds are nearly
completely blank about the relative role of junctions in
road accidents, as opposed to carriageways. Both these
examples are real problems - we need to endeavour to do

quite a lot better on traffic accident analysis, because I
believe it is both possible and important (in contrast to
other needs which one can readily identify for data, to
continue my sceptical theme, but which it is effectively
impossible to satisfy in practice). We must also do better
with respect to regularly weighing axles, because there is
strong evidence of abuse here, with consequential high
costs to the community. The integrated use of dynamic
weighbridges should help here, but like many such devices
these have to be properly integrated with policy and its
overall management to reap their rewards - something that
I feel cannot be too strongly stressed. The direction is
thus decidedly towards requiring rather more data, at a
greater degree of disaggregation, and thus the major theme
of this Conference of automatic traffic data collection is
very timely. There is also a need, which the TRRL have in
hand, for a cheap, foolproof and readily transportable(!)
indicator of the standard axle passes that could be used
by local authorities to indicate the amount of heavy traffic
on the more minor roads: it is this heavy traffic, to
repeat, that causes the damage, and for which at present
there is no systematic method of measurement.

12. Thus I have said a moderate amount about traffic flow,
and the need for greater disaggregation, and mentioned in
passing accidents and axle loads. The catalogue of needs
certainly does not stop there: for instance, for road
safety purposes it would be desirable to have continuous
indicators of vehicle speeds and headways on some national
average basis. And without difficulty any of us could
readily extend such a catalogue of needs. But as I have
indicated, there is a limit to this, to what can be undertaken at any time. The most important needs at the present
time, as I see them, are for improving our framework for our
traffic _flow_ data collection, the introduction of more automatic data collection within this framework to give flow
categorisation by vehicle type, and the general improvement
of our accident information and analysis. That is quite
enough to be going on with.

Personal Views on Limitations

13. We must recognise that aspirations towards comprehensive data banks are dangerous, that the belief that the
world can be better organised through a comprehensive
management information system is perfectionist stupidity.
The attractions of such beliefs are apparent and felt by all
of us, but they are founded on an erroneous philosophy.

Let me put down a contrary set of hypotheses, to see
whether you would not rather believe these:

a. We can never foresee all the information that will
be needed in the future. The world we live in is
always changing, and the future is essentially unknown;

b. We can never identify all the information that is
either desired or desirable;

c. We can never get all the information that we
identify as required;

d. We can never perfectly store and access all the
information we have got;

e. We cannot perfectly analyse all the information to
which we have access;

We must remember that data is essentially artificial, our
own artefact and not something given by God. We forget
when we impose our tight specifications on data, which we
see as professionally necessary in order to import
precision, that what we are doing is distorting the real
world of our address, and not simply manifesting it. Thus
the analytical form that we adopt, for data collection and
its analysis, imposes a coherence on the world, at some
expense of the fullness of detail of the particular reality.
In short, we are playing professional games, and let us not
forget it.

14. This should not however be used to label me as a total
sceptic on the subject of our Conference, but more properly
to open our minds to what is impossible, namely a
perfection of data and its collection. There is, I am
sure, a way forward combining a better but fairly simple
framework for traffic flow data collection, that is
flexible enough to serve as a carrier for a variety of
other traffic data needs. But those are easy words to say - the
challenge to us all is to find the right way of giving them
effect.

3. Traffic data for highway design and appraisal

M.F. Maggs, BSc, CEng, MICE, FIMunE, F Inst HE
Department of Transport

SYNOPSIS. Highway design and appraisal methodology is
heavily dependent upon traffic flow data obtained mainly
from automatic traffic counters. For large network
studies the demand for link flow data is very considerable
and the data used is often referenced to different time
periods that makes a detailed knowledge of seasonal and
hourly variations essential. At the present time
available data is not sufficient to support link flow
estimates based on short term counts and a concept is
proposed that would make this possible. Design and
appraisal parameters do not share a common reference flow
characteristic and it is proposed that annual average
daily flow should be used as the common reference
parameter.

INTRODUCTION

1. The design and appraisal of both major and minor
inter urban highway projects requires a great deal of data
concerning the traffic that will use the proposed scheme.
Some of these data will be specific to the highway under
consideration and required as input to the design
standards, while other data will have been established
previously in order to formulate these standards. Finally
a further set of data will be needed after the construction
of the highway, to check both its performance in meeting
the design objectives, and to check whether the
assumptions remain valid over time. This latter data
collection exercise is termed monitoring and is carried out
on both a local and national basis.

2. The type of data used for design and appraisal are
collected from various sources including:

1. origin and destination roadside surveys
2. classified traffic counts over various periods
3. automatic traffic counts over various periods
4. link speed surveys at various flow levels
5. household travel surveys
6. population surveys
7. employment surveys
8. commercial goods surveys.

3. The conference is concerned only with the collection of traffic flow data, and this paper is therefore addressed to the use of automatically collected traffic data in the design and appraisal of highway schemes. A great variety of data can now be collected by automatic recording equipment but at the present time most of the data used for design and appraisal will have been obtained from automatic recording of total traffic volumes using roadside counters, or will have been factored or otherwise modified by data obtained from counters.

DESIGN STANDARDS

4. In order that highway schemes should be designed on a nationally consistent basis utilising research and previous experience for both safety and economy to the best advantages, the Department of Transport promulgates Design Standards which it requires to be used as the basis for the design of its trunk road schemes. There are six main areas of the design process where design standards require information from automatic traffic counts as input.

Scale of capacity provision

5. The capacity provision i.e. a dual carriageway, or motorway etc, is assessed by the methodology of Technical Memorandum H6/74 which draws a distinction between those roads that sustain high levels of flow for short time periods and those that experience a more even flow of traffic throughout the "16 hour day" - 0600 hours to 2200 hours. There are therefore two requirements: (1) an estimate of 16 hour average daily flow in the month during which the heaviest traffic levels occur (most likely August), (2) peak hour : daily flow ratio - PDR - defined as the highest flow for any specific hour of the week averaged over any consecutive 13 weeks during the busiest period of the year. This requires the measurement of hourly flows of at least five three day periods during the peak season June to September and over three of four

consecutive hours spanning the peak hours on these days.

Commercial vehicles

6. Obviously in all design standards, the effect of
heavy commercial vehicles must have a greater impact than
that of a private car or light van. At present because
no means exist of automatically classifying commercial
traffic on the scale required for design, design standards
assume a constant proportion of heavy goods vehicles in the
total traffic flow mix. In the case of H6/74 this is 15%
although adjustments are made for variants from this and
it is therefore necessary to make an assessment of commercial traffic in excess of 15%.

Junction design

7. Junctions are designed to handle streams of traffic
that are in conflict, competing with each other for the
same road space. Design is therefore related to the most
severe conflict flow conditions that can be expected to
occur and assessment of flows at peak hour is therefore
needed. Assessments will usually be based or draw heavily
upon counts of turning movements taken during peak
conditions, often for periods of much less than an hour's
duration.

Economic evaluation

8. In assessing the economic return obtained from a
particular highway investment the Department's cost
benefit analysis program COBA calculates the net present
value of the investment by discounting capital costs and
benefits over a thirty year assessment period. Inherent
requirements of these procedures are measurements of
average daily flow in the peak month on every link of the
network influenced by the scheme; some hundreds of link
flows have to be measured by means of counters for every
scheme evaluated. Assumptions have to be made about the
hourly distribution of traffic flow throughout the day and
the seasonal variation of daily flow throughout the year.
These distributions have been assessed on a national
average basis using national census data but they are
known to vary considerably according to the particular
function of the road in its local context and the
assumption of a single national average in the absence of
anything else is a defect of present procedures.

Paper 3: Maggs

Environmental assessment

9. The assessment of traffic noise is determined from estimates of traffic flow over an 18 hour (0600 - 2400 hours) weekday during the busiest month of the year using a fixed proportion of heavy goods vehicles.

Pavement design

10. The structural design of the highway pavement is related to the estimated flow of commercial vehicles from which the total number of standard axle passes occurring throughout the fifteen year design period is calculated. Data on the daily and seasonal variation of commercial vehicles is needed for this.

11. It can be seen from the preceeding description of design standards that automatic traffic count data is required to establish the following time based relationships.

1. 16 hour (06.00 - 22.00) flow ↔ 24 hour flow
2. 18 hour (06.00 - 24.00) flow ↔ 24 hour flow
3. Average Weekday (Mon - Fri) ↔ Average 7 day week
4. Average busiest monthly day (and August)
5. Average peak hour over busiest three months
6. Seasonal variation characteristics of car and commercial vehicular traffic.

DESIGN STANDARD PHILOSOPHY

12. The time based relationships in current design standards are not necessarily related to technical considerations. August has been for many years the peak month of the year for traffic, though this has been changing in some aspects in recent years, but apart from this characteristic, the choice of August as a standard for observations has other advantages. It is an easy period in which to conduct major traffic surveys because in the holiday period many students are available to act as enumerators, furthermore the sixteen hour survey period, 6 a.m. to 10 p.m., corresponds roughly to the hours of daylight allowing for observations to be carried out in comparative safety, and with reasonable prospects of good weather. However, there is no absolute requirement for surveys to be carried out in August, but only that data are available from which peak month flows can be estimated from surveys or counts at any other time of the year.

22

This means that flow data has to be obtained first to ablish which month is peak month and second to establish n peak hour flows occur in order that the flows can then counted. It will be readily conceded that our design ndards and methodology are not based on any single data ionale. The situation is apparently further compounded the need to adapt or convert the output of traffic els, (which normally provide estimates of annual average ly flow), to design standard parameter forms. However, s begs the question that present parameter forms are most appropriate.

The adoption of average annual daily flow as the ndard reference characteristic would greatly facilitate ign processes and enable ready conversions to be made any other flow characteristic. Furthermore it would e design less influenced by the peculiar characteristics August itself such as its holiday and school trip terns. The average annual day concept is by nature e robust in relation to such external influences. In ition as many of the surveys are now carried out at er times of the year, mainly between April and October, conversion of these data to an August base probably ls to greater inaccuracy than would conversion to ual average daily flow. The Department is developing an roach to the use of average annual daily traffic as the non reference for its design standards.

EME EVALUATION PROCEDURES

The preceding sections of this paper have centrated on the design standards which exist for the raisal and design of highway schemes. The procedures lowed in designing a highway and the use that is made traffic count data needs further elaboration to onstrate their importance and the significance of data lity.

For the evaluation of any new highway scheme, the vork of roads that will be affected by the introduction a new scheme has to be determined and this is termed study network. This network without the new scheme termed the do-nothing network and the network with the scheme in is termed the do-something network. Cordon screen line origin and destination surveys carried out ing the survey period (any convenient time during the ths April to October) provide the basic data for a ssignment of trips from the do-nothing network to the

23

do-something network. The cordons and screenlines are
drawn to intercept all trips likely to use a new road
facility, and thus provide the data from which the peak
month flows on it can be estimated. These surveys however
do not intercept and record all the flows on the study
network within the cordon crossing points. This network
includes roads and junctions whose flow levels will be
both reduced and increased by reassignments and it is
necessary to estimate what these changes will be in order
to calculate the total benefits gained from the scheme
being evaluated.

17. The link flows within the cordon are obtained from
automatic traffic counts, together with counts of turning
movements at significant junctions. The appraised
networks for large highway schemes such as motorways are
extensive and the amount of counting required to establish
these flows properly is enormous. Consequently it is often
the practice to use whatever historical data exists,
factoring this upwards and filling the gaps with new count
data as necessary. The extent of this counting and the
availability of counting equipment inevitably stretches
these counting operations over a long period of time.
There are therefore problems of temporal reconciliation,
not only between new and old data but also between new
data. There has finally to be a reconciliation between
survey period data and design standards.

18. Reconciliations between differing time periods
should be based upon local records if these exist. Often
they do not and the only source available is that contained
in "Traffic Prediction for Rural Roads" published by DTp
in 1968 which reproduces average variations drawn from
1963 based data. Clearly this procedure is highly unsatisfactory and may lead to substantial error in the
evaluation calculations.

19. To summarise, automatic traffic counting is required
for each scheme design and appraisal as follows:

    a) to relate each origin and destination survey
        station data to an average survey period -
        normally 7 days continuous counting before and
        after the station survey dates.

    b) to relate each survey period to peak month for
        capacity design.

    c) to relate each survey period to August for COBA
        input.

d) to ascertain the total flows on each link of the COBA network.

e) to relate new link counts and historical counts to present day August flows.

f) to ascertain turning movements at significant junctions.

g) to relate junction flows to peak month and to August.

DATA SOURCES

20. Other papers describe in detail the present national data sources and discuss future proposals for national traffic censuses in this country; these have a particular relevance to scheme appraisal and design because so much of design methodology and policy is based upon data obtained from these sources.

21. The primary source of continuous ATC data in this country is the TRRL 50 point census. However of the 50 sites only 9 are situated on the major inter urban highway network in England, hence decisions and estimates based upon factors derived from this census do not carry conviction when applied to the trunk road network, though there are a number of additional points covering motorways. Within the 200 point census, there are estimated to be 27 points on motorways, 34 points on trunk roads and 79 points on principal roads on the major inter urban highway network and so further data can be drawn from this source. However by far the major source at present of ATC data is the county councils, who for various reasons carry out numerous ATC counts throughout their areas. At present these are of varying duration and quality and are presented in differing formats; never the less they are extremely valuable data sources that are not exploited nationally.

22. One other major source of data used in scheme appraisal is the General Traffic Census (GTC). The GTC is essentially a manual vehicle classified count carried out on a consecutive Sunday and Monday from 6 a.m. to 10 p.m. in late July or August and a quarter of the points are counted again in the following April or May. The survey covers some 6,300 points on motorways, trunk and principal roads throughout Great Britain.

23. These data are used in scheme appraisal for the following purposes:

a) assessing network stress and identifying problem
   links requiring improvement.

b) estimating "busiest month" 16 hour flows for input
   to design standards when a specific location
   survey is not possible.

c) estimating the proportion of commercial vehicles
   and input data for design and economic appraisal.

d) traffic monitoring (discussed later in this paper).

24. A number of criticisms can be made of the GTC.
Firstly counts are taken in anticipation of need rather
than when required, which means the proportion of unused
data is high; this also means that some data will be
considerably out of date when it is used. Further,
because the count is made in August, large errors may
occur when factoring to other time periods because of the
lack of seasonal variation information. Finally, because
casual labour is used the error in counting and recording
is thought to be high. Taking all things into account the
GTC is a poor source of data that is totally inadequate
for design and appraisal purposes. It appears to be used
because it exists and because there is no other readily
available source of link flow data on the same scale.

25. The use of the GTC in this way highlights an important
area for future development. As scheme appraisal increases
in sophistication, and in particular with the introduction
of the Regional Highway Traffic Model, it is vital that
data relating to the seasonal variation of traffic flow
should be more robust and be collected by vehicle type.
Due to the length of count required this can only be done
by using automatic equipment, and it is to be hoped the
work at present being carried out on the development of
automatic vehicle classification systems by number of axles,
weight etc will make possible the collection of much more
classified data.

MONITORING

26. It was this shortage of data on the use of the major
inter urban network accentuated by the development of the
Regional Highway Traffic Model that prompted Traffic
Engineering Division to establish in 1977 approximately
120 permanent ATC sites, all of which are situated on the
major inter urban highway network in England embracing
wherever possible appropriate existing 200 point census

sites. Each site provides continuous 24 hour, 7 days a week, data collected by automatic counter linked to pneumatic tube or loop detector, and already over one years continuous data is available from all sites.

27. With the assistance of other divisions in the Department of Transport a manual of Automatic Traffic Counting Practice was prepared and a number of computer programs written to ensure that all the data are collected, corrected and stored to a common high standard. These data will be used for the following purposes:

a) to provide data for the derivation and updating of traffic parameters used in the design standards.

b) to provide a more satisfactory basis of assessing link flow characteristics from short term counts.

c) to monitor change in respect of flow variation used for the Regional Highway Traffic Model.

28. Information collected from these 120 ATC sites should enable more accurate estimates of seasonal variation to be made. As has been previously stated the current seasonal variation of traffic flow estimates are made using nationally derived factors produced in 1963. The seasonal variation in traffic flow is caused by variation in both journey length and trip purpose throughout the year. For example it is unlikely that the number of journeys to work will vary much throughout the year; but of course they actually fall during the summer holiday period. The number of journeys for leisure and recreational purposes however obviously increase during the summer months as do the length of such journeys. Investigation is currently being carried out to see if there are groups of roads which exhibit certain similar patterns in seasonal variation. It seems likely that four main categories of road function may exist for this purpose each with its own seasonal characteristics.

1. Holiday and recreational routes
2. Long distance trunk roads
3. Urban commuter routes
4. Other mainly rural roads.

29. If functional categorisation is valid it may be possible to group all roads in the inter urban highway network into one of these above categories. Then by using the results from a short term automatic traffic count it would be possible to arrive at an estimated

annual flow within calculable ranges of accuracy.

ACCURACY OF DATA

30. One of the main criticisms levelled at current design procedures, and in particular the use of automatic traffic counts is that it has not been possible to state the accuracy of the data. Even the most meticulously maintained traffic counters fail for a variety of reasons and it is rare indeed for any counter to achieve a greater than 90% recording record over a long period. Far more difficult is the problem of under counting due to some counter malfunction when a plausible recording is still made. Such problems can mean that the confidence limits for a traffic count over a short period are at best $\pm$ 20%. An advantage of the classification system proposed in the previous section is that it would then enable estimates of the confidence limits of a short term count to be made, by relating it to a continuous station exhibiting similar patterns of seasonal behaviour, though actual vehicle flow cannot be measured precisely and it may not be possible to do so in the forseeable future.

31. The effect of these basic data errors, which subsequent papers will describe more fully, together with errors resulting from current design techniques and design standards make decisions on standards of provision of road very difficult to make and even more difficult to defend against public criticism. These problems can only be overcome by a combination of improved traffic counting equipment, better education of the users of such equipment and design standards that recognise the limitations of the data used to forecast traffic flows.

32. The improved education of the users of automatic traffic counting equipment is perhaps one of the most important and immediate remedies open to us at this time. All too often the maintenance and inspection of traffic counters is left to technicians with little knowledge of the use to which the data is put and little if any awareness of how critical it may be to the design and evaluation decisions that it influences. Since the work is so fundamental to the design process it merits the oversight of more senior staff and it may be that the traffic counter manufacturers can assist by offering more guidance on the maintenance of their machines.

CONCLUSIONS

33. The design and appraisal of highway schemes require a great deal of data from automatic traffic counts. The accuracy of count data has an important bearing on scheme design and evaluation.

34. Data available from national sources do not provide a robust basis for scheme use in relation to seasonal variations or factoring requirements.

35. Local authority sources of flow data are probably quite extensive and collectively constitute a potential source of data that could be exploited regionally and nationally if collected in accordance with a national standard system.

36. The responsibility for data collection and the inspection of counting installations should be entrusted to properly trained technical staff and under the supervision of qualified engineering staff responsible for ensuring data quality.

37. Design standard parameters could be rationalised by adoption of a common reference basis.

Discussion on Papers 1, 2 and 3

Mr Fry (Paper 1)

Since this paper was written, the thinking of the Department
of the Environment on the system of traffic data collection
it needs has made further progress. The scheme now
envisaged would reduce the present four traffic censuses to
two. One would be a new version of the monthly 200-point
census which would be totally automated using advanced
microprocessor-based equipment of considerable versatility.
It would serve not only the statistical functions of the
present census, but would in time provide the continuous monitoring needed for the Regional Highway Traffic Models; and
would provide the potential for measurement of speed, distance
between vehicles, and axle loads.
The second census would be a large rotating sample which
over a period of 5 years would cover 6000 sites on the
English road network. It would provide the required statistical benchmark for national trends in traffic, and also the
range of link-specific counts required for various purposes.
Automation of this census would be desirable but would
require development of reliable mobile counters.
The new scheme represents the first step in what should be
a process of steady development in response to changing needs.
The consultation with local government should not be superficial. Local and central data collection activities need to
be jointly developed so as to mutually support total national
requirements. Some of the data organization features of this
scheme would serve those ends.

Mr Maggs (Paper 3)

I am concerned that national censuses are not structured to
provide the information needed for design and as a result
capacity design methodology is based upon an unsatisfactory

parameter: the peak to daily flow ratio PDR. It has been found that the error around the estimate PDR is at least as large as the range of PDRs found in practice. This means that the Memorandum H6/74[1.1] concept of tailoring design to match local flow characteristics cannot be sustained.

Flow characteristics vary enormously from site to site, daily through the week and seasonally through the year. Road side surveys and counts undertaken for scheme appraisal occur within a jungle of patterns and the larger the network studied, the denser the jungle. Conversion factors have to be derived to convert the sample to survey day, to average survey month, to peak (or design) month, to August (for COBA). No framewok of local censuses exists to endow such factors with statistical credentials. The calculation of link flows on a COBA network by subtracting do-something assignments, obtained from cordon surveys, from intra cordon counts is heavily dependent upon the validity of the counts. With COBA benefits very sensitive to the flow values used, particularly at junctions, the validity of the economic appraisal is contingent upon the accuracy of the actual counts and the validity of the factors used. Many schemes pass or fail the positive NPV criterion according to the rules of chance.

The Department is concerned that the standards and practice for automatic counting are generally unsatisfactory particularlay in regard to continuous counting or counting over long periods where rigorous surveillance of counters is essential to obtain data of a satisfactory quality. Much count data collected from county sources for the Department's flow analysis was unusable because of missing periods, obvious counter malfunction, or coding error all of which demonstrated a clear need for a new approach to management and direction of counting activities with more professional engineer input. The routine nature of traffic counting leads to a low level of engineer oversight and direction in which the engineer input is required to construct and maintain a statistical framework for counting within determinable confidence levels. The Department and local Authorities should work together within an integrated statistical framework of local and national censuses interfacing to improve the quality of data used. Furthermore this need cost no more money and might well reduce total expenditure on counting.

In conclusion I would like to draw attention to some of the hardware problems experienced by the Department in obtaining rapid reading facilities from translator unit to terminal to mainframe computer. After more than a year of endeavours leading suppliers of counting equipment and computer terminals have not produced a solution and while the Department have pre-contract consultations with both I feel that the counter manufacturers and computer suppliers are not themselves in dialogue identifying and solving compatability problems and the customer remains poorly served though the equipment is otherwise excellent. I am especially concerned that the next generation of processing equipment, which would be at a higher level of sophistication again, should not suffer from lack of awareness of system requirements.

Mr S. E. Evans (LGORU, Reading)

I have a number of brief points to make concerning Mr Maggs' Paper.

We at LGORU have done some work for the Department of Transport on seasonal adjustment factors and brought them up to date to 1974-75. If counts in April and May are taken, a stable relationship with the annual flow can be seen. This is also true of counts taken in October but to a lesser extent than in April/May. Although I endorse some of Mr Maggs' points about the variability of seasonal adjustment factors between sites, this can be lessened if counts are taken in April or May rather than in August.

Mr Maggs suggests categorizing sites by perhaps four types and deriving seasonal adjustment factors for them. I am sure that would be correct, but it leads to problems of classifying sites for a COBA analysis and opens up the temptation to the traffic engineer to choose the category most favourable for his particular argument. As an alternative it should be possible to classify sites by the journey purpose mix, which would for example indicate whether there is a recreational aspect to the site or not.

Mr K. Sriskandan (Department of Transport)

There is an aspect of traffic data which is not mentioned in the papers - traffic data for bridge loading purposes. Bridges are designed to carry a distributed load which varies with the span, and represents normal traffic loading. In order to specify this distributed loading it is necessary to know the axle loading, axle spacings and vehicle weight of individual vehicles and also the actual mix of vehicles and the headway between them. This information is required not for just one lane in a carriageway but coincident loadings in other lanes are also required.

Weighbridge measurements will give axle weights and number
of axles making up one vehicle. From this and information
from vehicle manufacturers it has been possible to derive
axle spacings. However, measurement of headways are not
available.

Another problem is that the axle loads measured by weighbridges installed in a carriageway lane are dynamic weights.
In a small span bridge the worst effects are probably caused
by a single heavy vehicle and dynamic weights are what are
required. In the case of a large span bridge however the
effects are at their worst when a large number of heavy
vehicles are closely bunched together as in a standstill condition. Under these circumstances, static axle loads and
corresponding headways are required.

It is hoped that measurements taken by TRRL, and photographs of vehicles in standstill conditions will help in
determining headways. Static axle loadings may be more difficult to obtain and some assumptions may need to be made
about the relationship between static and the measured
dynamic axle weights.

Dr J.D.G.F. Howe (Alastair Dick and Associates)

There are two problems that are rarely discussed which need
to be overcome if the hopes for better traffic flow estimates are to be realized.

The first is the need to tidy up the definition of what it
is one is trying to estimate when talking about traffic parameters for planning and design. Many are, when closely
examined, loosely defined. For example the wording of the
Memorandum H6/74[1.1] is such that it is possible to derive from
the same data three quite separate values for the quantity
peak hourly flow. These will on average differ by about 20%.
In the case of a recreational holiday route it can be very
much more than that.

Another ambiguity is in COBA's description of the M factor.
It confusingly describes the constant H in the relationship
either as the proportion of 'heavy vehicles' or the proportion of 'heavy goods vehicles . This is repeated in the
Leitch Committee Report.[1.2] In general highway engineering
and traffic engineering parlance the term heavy vehicles and
heavy goods vehicles have separate meanings. Using them in
an M factor relationship would give different values. Most
traffic parameters are described in terms of things such as
peak flows, averages and busiest periods and those terms are
very rarely defined.

Thus a significant proportion of the variability in present
traffic estimates is really caused by the looseness of the

definitions, and no change in methodology or sampling or
shifting from April to May will make any difference. Further
any attempt to produce better or optimum methods is likely
to be defeated, by reason of the simple fact that in comparing method A with method B, unless there is some fixed
method of measurement, there is no means of knowing what the
difference between them is due to.

With regard to Mr Fry's paper it seems that we need a much
better machinery for making quickly and widely available the
data that we already produce and incorporating it into decision making.

The problems caused by the use of a single notational factor in relation to seasonal variation are compounded by the
fact that the data are based on the years 1963-64. This
data is used not because current values do not exist, they
do, but little official use is made of them. What is
basically at fault is that there is an administrative procedure which produces traffic estimating relationships such as
the M factor, tables of seasonal variation and many others,
but only intermittently, whereas most traffic measures are
in a fairly continuous process of change. What is required
is a change of attitude. There should be an annual review
and updating as necessary of all relationships for estimating traffic flows. This is important with regard to all
traffic flow estimation relationships used for making basic
decisions.

The Leitch Committee did not appear to probe deeply into
the question of the sensitivity of the COBA relationship to
errors in present traffic estimates, but on p106 of the Leitch
Committee Report [1,2] it says ' We suspect that the sensitivity of COBA to the estimates is at least as great as
uncertainties in forecasting'. This must be the case
because the cost benefit appraisal technique is one in which
there is an inbuilt safeguard against future forecast errors,
the costs and benefits are discounted with time. Present-day
traffic estimates are not discounted. Therefore it is quite
easy to show that 100% error in a traffic forecast for a
design year is no more sensitive to a cost benefit appraisal
than a 30% error in the present day traffic estimates which
is quite common.

Mr E. W. Smith (Department of Transport)

I should like to discuss a few examples of some traffic data
collection exercises carried out by the Department in the
South West, their needs and the use to which they were put.
A short- and medium-term exercise monitoring the effects

of network changes from the period 1968-77 was carried out.
The South-West is ideally placed for screen line surveys as
one can be put across the peninsula and be covered with 7
stations.

There are two particular routes, the A38 used before the
M5 was completed, and the A30 linking the A303 to London.
There was an exceptional growth across the peninsula concen-
trated on the A38 which was caused by traffic generated by
the M5. The main use is in analysing the A30 and A303; and
it demonstates the dangers of counting there, surveying in
isolation and how misleading answers can be obtained if the
wrong time is chosen for the survey. Memorandum H6/7.4[1.1]
brought about the need to look at flow variations as well as
the average august day. Reference was made to recreational
routes such as the A30 and the A303 and it was implied that
about 200 hours could safely be exceeded above what was
termed the standard peak hour capacity. The number of hours
and number of days when certain flow levels were exceeded
was looked at compared with different days in order to see
what ought to be the design day or the design hour. The survey data was also examined. The origin and destination survey used here was a week day, a Tuesday which was considered
to be a fairly typical week day. Saturday was also chosen and
in trying to convert those two days into an average day,
information from automatic traffic counters was used to convert the survey first to average August week day and
Saturday.

The M5 was constructed and opened as it went along and
there was one hole in the middle of it at the Avonmouth
bridge for over a year. During that period traffic routed
itself in a variety of ways from the northern to the
Sommerset part of the M5. The regional office of the
Department of Transport sponsored a before and after study
consisting of 12 automatic traffic counters on seven sites
with the idea of monitoring the effect of the opening of the
bridge on the network for two weeks before and after. The
information needed by an engineer to plan and design a road
is fairly minimal. The information that was provided 5 or
10 years ago was much less than it is now. Despite all the
extra data that is collected, it is doubtful whether design
offices, counties or RCU sub-units are getting a better service from their traffic sections now. However the same
engineer probably needs more information in order to justify
a project to his fellow professionals whose brief is some-
what different. Furthermore the engineer needs an enormous
supply of information to answer any question that will arise

in regard to road schemes. Alongside this there is also the
general monitoring which goes on in terms of accident data
and traffic trends. When considering cost-effectiveness of
data collection we have to look at the criteria and who sets
them.

Mr I. Harrison (Kent County Council)

Mr Maggs has explained the difficulty of categorizing roads,
and has provided a good example of a computer route with
recreational overtones.

Kent County Council are concerned with road categorization,
and have adopted an approach which brings together data collected from two sources, traffic counts and roadside interviews; the latter giving information about trip purpose. In
Kent we have tried to derive, from sites which have both
automatic count records and roadside interviews, a profile
of seasonal variation for each trip purpose. We found insufficient sites which met this specification, and have therefore approached other counties for data, throught the
STLDC's.

Fig. 1.1 shows the initial results obtained in the form of
monthly variation profiles for five trip purposes and
vehicle types. Non-recreational trips, such as work and
shopping, show a fairly even pattern throughout the year,
with a drop in August. Recreational trips show a sharp peak
in August, whereas there are few educational trips in that
month. Commercial vehicle movements show less variation,
although medium and heavy goods trips show a drop in mid-
summer.

The mathematical model used to produce these profiles is
based on the hypothesis that the purpose variation patterns
are universal at all sites. The differences in the overall
flow patterns observed at traffic counter sites result from
differences in the mix of traffic at those sites. As the
basic data source for the model is automatic counter records,
the variations are a measure of change in vehicle mileage,
and therefore represent seasonal variations in both numbers
of trips and trip length.

With such information about the variations by trip purpose,
for any particular road (i.e. purpose mix) a profile of variation of the total flow of traffic on that road type throughout the year can be obtained.

Five types of road are shown in Fig. 1.2. At the top is the
most stable flow pattern, an urban road. Moving through
inter-urban and rural roads to those with progressively
greater components of holiday and recreational traffic, the
magnitude of seasonal variation increases.

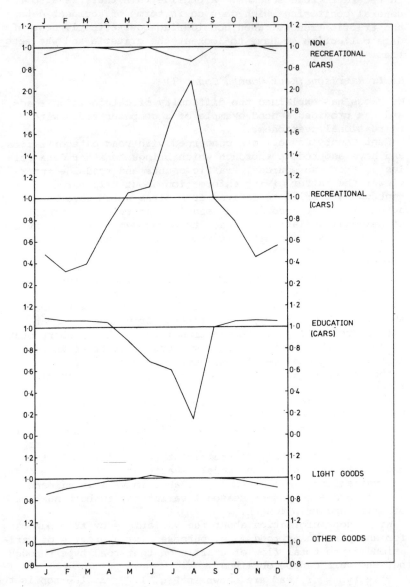

Fig. 1.1. Monthly profiles for grouped purposes

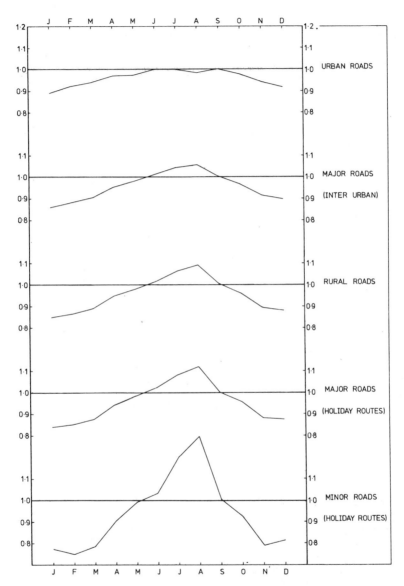

'ig. 1.2. Monthly flow variations for different road types
        (September = 1.0)

Discussion on Papers 1, 2 and 3

The method allows the derivation of seasonal flow variation for any type of road (i.e. purpose mix), and therefore
does not require rigid categorization. If purpose variations are ignored, and seasonal changes are predicted with
reference to a set of automatic counters for specified road
categories, considerable errors could be found. To illustrate this, Fig. 1.3 shows the example of a roadside interview
site at post 'A'. This intercepts traffic going to two
places, to 'B', an industrial area and to 'C', a holiday
resort. At the June interview period, there is a mix of 500
holiday trips, and 2000 non-holiday trips, but this must be
factored to the August (peak month) flow for use in COBA.
Factoring by purpose profile gives an August flow of 3000,
split evenly between holiday trips to 'C', and industrial
trips to 'B', whereas a reference automatic counter would
suggest the same August total 3000, with the bias of trips
to the industrial area retained.

Looking at the August flows on this road network, both
systems of factoring give the same flow of 3000 between 'A'
and 'B'. However, on the section between 'B' and 'C',
widely differing predictions result, 1500 by purpose factors
and 600 by direct reference to a control counter at A.

This stylized example is exaggerated, but the implication
is that care must be taken when using automatic counters to
predict seasonal variation. A model incorporating purpose
variations, as I have described, would seem to be more satisfactory, if it can be calibrated with statistical confidence.

Mr P. W. Davies (Department of Transport)

In the Department of Transport the formula $M = 233 + 5.7H$
has been used for aggregating traffic. The H is normally
taken to be vehicles with over $1\frac{1}{2}$ tons unladen weight, but
it is more complicated than that, for example, it is neces-
say for speed flow purposes to record vehicles with more
than 4 wheels. However the fortunate position is that we
in the Department now have a better means of aggregating
traffic, and this involves a simple number relating to a
particular month. This is based on a study, carried out
under the Department's direction, by the Local Government
Operational Research Unit. It also follows from the study
that the variation in the M-factor is statistically less in
April than in other months, so it would be my recommendation
that traffic be counted in this month.

Where national versus local trends are concerned a national
trend should be defined, and it is for local areas or users
to suggest a departure from that national trend, and to make

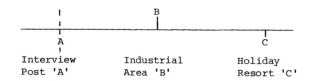

June Interview   :-   Non Holiday Trips to 'B'   =   2000
at 'A'   Holiday Trips to 'C'   =   500
                                                       2500

Let $\dfrac{\text{August}}{\text{June}}$ Purpose Factors be -   Non Holiday Trips   0.75
                                                 Holiday Trips   3.00

∴ By purpose factoring, predicted August flows at 'A'

   Non Holiday Trips to 'B' = 2000 x 0.75 = 1500
   Holiday Trips to 'C'   = 500 x 3.0   = 1500
                                            3000

∴   Link flows 'A' - 'B' = 3000
               'B' - 'C' = 1500

$\dfrac{\text{August}}{\text{June}}$ factor from ATC at 'A' = $\dfrac{3000}{2500}$ = 1.20

By reference counter, predicted August flows at 'A'

   Non Holiday Trips at 'B' = 2000 x 1.20 = 2400
   Holiday Trip to 'C'   = 500 x 1.20 = 600
                                            3000

∴   Link flows 'A' - 'B' = 3000
               'B' - 'C' = 600

Fig. 1.3. Example of possible errors

allowance for it as necessary. But the problem is very complicated. Not only are we interested in the aggregated annual totals but also the variation of traffic flows throughout the year and for COBA purposes we have four hourly flow groups which are indicated by blocks, as can be seen from Fig. 1.4.

In the South-West a pattern is emerging that is probably more like the dotted line in the figure. This indicates that we have less traffic out of the holiday times and more traffic, and thus a greater peak effect, in the particular holiday months such as in August. The Local Government Operational Research Unit study has indicated that the area underneath the curve which gives the total volume of travel can reasonably be estimated, although the shape may vary.

The main problems arise in estimating the variations in the peak. Traffic flow is not the only variable, for evaluation purposes it is necessary to consider occupancies and values of time. In the holiday areas it can be argued that the value of time is less, therefore the economic worth of travel is also less, so that overall the average may be restored to within the national pattern, for evaluation purposes.

Delays at junctions and more reliable measurements of these is now a concern. There again, the same approach in indicating, particularly to users of COBA, the national parameters that we intend to use will have to be adopted, and it will be for them to demonstrate in their particular cases the variations from the national, so that if necessary allowance can be made for them.

Mr H. Williams (Department of Transport)

Road safety has not been discussed specifically and I would like to consider some work done by TRRL on lane distribution, which has been related to traffic flows given in the Memorandum H6/74[1].[1]

The maximum flow laid down per lane for peak hour design purposes was 1,600 vehicles per hour and distribution was assumed to be equal across each lane. With that flow, at a speed of about 70 miles per hour, the standard recommended headway distance, as recommended in the Highway Code, which is equivalent in terms of time to two seconds, would be obtained. The work which TRRL has done on the distribution of the flow on traffic lanes on M4 during the peak hours has shown that as traffic builds up from a fairly modest flow in which most of the traffic is in the slow lane, more and more traffic uses the centre lane and most traffic uses

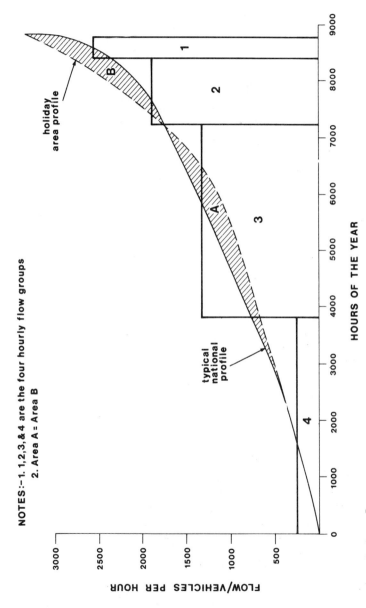

NOTES:- 1. 1,2,3,& 4 are the four hourly flow groups
2. Area A = Area B

holiday
area profile

typical
national
profile

FLOW/VEHICLES PER HOUR

HOURS OF THE YEAR

Fig. 1.4. Traffic flow levels

43

the right hand lane at periods of very high flow. Drivers not wanting to get trapped, i.e. unable to overake, should go into the right-hand lane.

The situation shown by the work done is that roughly over 2,000 vehicles per hour are using the fast lane when the average flow along the carriageway is 4,800 vehicles per hour. At that particular flow there is a 37% chance of there being less than one second headway between vehicles, which is very different from the two seconds assumed when the design flows were introduced. There is a higher potential of a serious accident occurring in this area because of those traffic flows. Data collection which gives this kind of information is very useful when one is dealing with possible new criteria which may be introduced when transferring to average annual daily flow for design purposes.

With regard to pavement design RRL Road Note 29 (third edition), produced in 1970, gave a method by which commercial vehicle flow would be converted by using certain conversion factors into the equivalent of standard axles, which were laid down as 8,200 kg. At that time, assumptions were made, based on experience, of the number of axles per commercial vehicle and the actual loading on each axle.

Since the fuel crises of 1973 it has been found that the number of axles per vehicle has risen and the average load per axle has increased. Presumably vehicles are being more economically loaded to reduce costs. What it means in terms of pavement design is that the make-up of the standard axles is now very much worse in terms of damaging power, because of the fourth power law, than was thought to be so when the Road Note was produced. It is therefore important to have information for construction purposes.

Dr J.G.M. Wood (Flint & Neill, Consulting Engineers)

The use of traffic data for the prediction of the extreme conditions which give the maximum load on a bridge requires careful treatment if events with probabilities of occurrence of once in 120 years are to be correctly predicted. Traffic as a whole does not follow the normal statistical distribution and the extreme event cannot be considered simply as the mean + n multiplied by the standard deviation.

However once the individual vehicles within the traffic stream are classified, as described in Paper 9, it is possible to produce a reasonably accurate model of the weight and length variation of each vehicle type. For the shortest bridges the load effects arise from a single vehicle and only the very heaviest vehicles need to be considered.

However with long span bridges the loading arises from

traffic in all lanes over lengths up to 1000 m. For these bridges the relative proportion of different classes of vehicles that can occur in any one event need to be considered for each lane. For this the data on the relative percentages of different types of vehicle and the percentage of laden vehicles within types is vital. The data being produced by TRRL described in Paper 9 is most valuable for this. On the M4 we have found that the hourly average percentage of commercial vehicles often rises 70 to 75% with greatly increased risk of long strings of laden lorries forming. Spacing between vehicles in free flowing conditions is unimportant but the spacings that can exist in queues of traffic at tolls, traffic lights or after accidents need to be accurately known.

Vehicle weight data from moving vehicles with impact effects is useful for classification and fatigue studies but it cannot be accurate enough by itself for a weight model. We have therefore supplemented it by records of overweight vehicles from County records.

Mr C.A. Cranley (Essex County Council)

Regarding resources, the national schemes represent less than 10% of my field work and 1% of my continuous field work. National data is old and predominantly rural.

As to cost, the local contributions added to the national contribution provide a substantial but insufficient sum. Trip rates, lengths, purposes, occupancy, alternative modes, pedestrians and bicycles, for instance are not covered.

With regard to equipment, there is a need for guidance on counters and sensors in setting up a local system and a classifier for congested urban roads for environmental traffic management or road safety matters.

Assuming one were to add up all existing expenditure and decide what could be done with it, utilizing all existing data with national co-ordination, research and developement, and assume that one were to bully counties to provide commitment and to encourage them by means of reimbursement, I suggest a figure nearer to 300% as compared with the local authorities cost plus 6%. Assume then that one were to take a system having a two-year moratorium on national counting, and to take the money and spend it on investigation, analysis and dissemination of existing data. There is a need for change and this could provide the resources.

There is a need for a reliable, indestructible, easily installed, non-mains axle detector. The loop configuration used for signal approaches where there is stationary, queueing traffic, gives a zero output most of the time.

Essex County Council have been attracted to the idea of
laying loops under resurfacing rather than slot cutting. On
a ten-year programme for resurfacing it would be possible to
install cheap loops throughout the county.

Mr D.H. Mathews (TRRL)

It is true that the seasonal variation factors are derived
from data that was gathered in 1963 and 1964 and based on the
50-point traffic census, plus the manual count which accom-
panied it at that stage. It has been said that these things
are out of date and that the position must have changed since
then.

We at TRRL did a detailed study of seasonal variation,
using our data bank, where for the whole of the 50-point
census we have 10 years of traffic flows on magnetic tape
which can be accessed immediately. There is surprisingly
little change from 1963-64. We have a new set of seasonal
variation factors, showing for inter-urban routes a remarkable
similarity with the old 1963 factors, and also a remarkable
agreement with the OLGORU work on M factors.

One therefore begins to wonder how big a problem it might
be to monitor what is going on. In my opinion it is not a
question of continual updating but of checking. At the same
time as the work mentioned was done we also estimated the
variability of our estimates. This is the vital thing. It
is not merely that they change in time but also a question
of how representative they are of roads in general? I think
this is Mr Cranley's problem. It is not the antiquity of the
National factors but the fact that for the roads he is looking at he is not using the best factors, i.e. those which
apply to his particular conditions.

On roads with a lot of commuters, the factors are not the
same as those for inter-urban roads, and on highly recreational roads, the factors would again be different. We at
the TRRL have arrived at a set of factors similar to those
suggested by Mr Maggs.

Mr Maggs (Paper 3)

I agree with Mr Evans that stable relationships are found
between annual flows and April/May counts, but this does not
solve the problem because one cannot always wait for April
or May to come around, and peak month flows need to be
counted as well. I also agree that we want to find an objective way of classifying sites and that journey purpose mix
might well be a useful discriminator if it can be deduced

and be predicted into the future, but the problems of doing this should not be underestimated.

Dr Howe emphasizes the need for tighter definitions of traffic design and evaluation parameters and I agree with his criticisms of H6/74[1.1] in this respect. One objective of the Department's work on flow characteristics is to review and revise the H6/74 methodology. I also agree with him that annual reviews and updating are essential and the Department has established flow monitoring procedures in order to do this. His point about the errors in present day traffic estimates and the sensitivity of the COBA evaluation to these estimates is a major one that is all to often over-looked by decision makers. A 30% error in the estimate of present day traffic would not be exceptional so he is right to point out that its effect upon the economic evaluation is equivalent to a 100% error in the design year forecast.

Mr Harrison's account of the work being done by Kent County Council on seasonal variation analysis and the categorization of roads is very promising.

It is interesting to learn from TRRL's work that national seasonal variation factors have shown little change since the question about how representative these national factors are to the particular roads we are designing or evaluating.

REFERENCES

1.1. Technical memorandum on design flows for motorways and rural all-purpose roads (Tecnical Memorandum H6/74) Department of the Environment, August, 1974.

1.2. Report of the advisory committee on trunk road assessment. (Chairman: Sir George Leitch). Department of Transport, (HMSO) London, October, 1977.

4. The local authority needs for traffic data and present methods of collection

V.E. Jones, MSc, DipTP, MICE, MIMunE, MIHE
Hereford and Worcester County Council

SYNOPSIS. Highway and pavement design, traffic and accident studies, economic assessment - these are just some of the applications of traffic data assembled by local authorities. This paper examines the traffic data requirements of county highways departments, and discusses the techniques, equipment and resources employed in data assembly.

1. INTRODUCTION

1.1 Local authorities require traffic data to carry out their extensive highway and planning functions. Such data are assembled by manual counting and by automatic means. In the urban areas, sophisticated land use - transportation studies which require large data inventories, aid decision taking by estimating the future demand for all forms of travel. This paper identifies the form and principal uses of traffic data and reviews the methods of assembly, drawing on the approaches adopted by a sample of shire and metropolitan counties.

1.2 The resources employed in collecting and analysing traffic data are significant and this aspect - which is of particular relevance at a time of financial stringency in public expenditure - is examined.

1.3 With economies in mind, there is scope for greater rationalisation of the concurrent censuses undertaken by the Department of Transport (D.Tp.) and local authorities and the implications of closer integration of these parallel and often overlapping activities are discussed.

2. DATA NEEDS OF LOCAL AUTHORITIES

2.1 Local authorities undertake regularly a number of traffic counts on behalf of the D.Tp. as part of the national censuses. These take the form of:

   (i) continuous traffic censuses such as the "50 point" automatic count. The coverage has recently been extended to include 120 sites on the national inter-urban highway network for regional highway traffic modelling purposes.

  (ii) a general traffic census (GTC) which relates to particular stretches of roads on the motorway, trunk and principal road network

 (iii) special sample censuses such as the "1300 point" benchmark census which estimates absolute traffic levels and the "200 point" monthly sample census which monitors national traffic trends.

2.2 Information from censuses such as the monthly "200 point" is helpful to local authorities and provides data on a long-time base for each census point which can be analysed to give:

   (i) annual and August 16 hour flows

  (ii) seasonal variation

 (iii) a guide to changes in vehicle-kms.

2.3 The degree of detail provided by these national road traffic censuses is generally much too coarse for local needs and the primary requirement of county highway authorities is for traffic information covering the whole network of trunk, principal and non-principal roads.

2.4 Data assembled in this way provide a quantified picture of the traffic using the roads in a county and forms the basis for delineating a functional hierarchy of routes for traffic, environmental and economic planning. The magnitude of any overloads on links in the network are highlighted immediately.

2.5 The extent of the coverage in this type of multi-point traffic census is determined by the availability of resources in terms of manpower and equipment. Sampling techniques are necessary and these relate to time and location.

2.6 In order to predict August average daily flow and annual flow for a range of errors between 5% and 25% the number of counters required is in the ratio 52 : 1 and most counties find it necessary to limit their activities to weekly counts at each site, and rely on additional monthly counts at sites on the trunk and principal roads to estimate seasonal variation. (ref.1).

Manual counts at a sub-set of the multi-point sites are generally taken during July and August to estimate traffic composition, and classified turning-counts at each main node in the network are also taken where resources permit.

2.7 The location of counting sites is based on positive selection, random selection or blanket coverage. The "100 point" census introduced by the Worcestershire County Council in 1969 used a modified stratified random sample to select sites. Hertfordshire County Council adopted a modified nodal blanket coverage to identify the 220 points used in its county traffic census.

2.8 Despite the increasing use of inductance loops as tripping devices for automatic traffic counters, most counties report difficulties in maintaining programme impetus due to resource limitations. Errors attributable to time sampling are compounded by those due to location sampling and care must be exercised in drawing inferences from traffic data assembled over a short time-base. Despite these limitations the multi-point county traffic censuses provide valuable data which can be augmented for most design purposes by local counts.

2.9 Having established a broad assessment of the pattern of travel on the highway network more specific data are required for the following design purposes:-

1. Transportation studies (including monitoring of predictions)

2. Economic evaluation

3. Design of highways - geometric
                       - junctions
                       - pedestrian facilities
                       - structural

4. Traffic noise estimation

5. Traffic management

6. Highway maintenance

7. Accident studies

8. Development control

These requirements are now considered in turn.

Transportation studies

2.10 During the past decade local authorities have undertaken major land use - transportation studies (LUTS) as an
aid to transport policy decisions. These studies call for
the following input data:-

(a) classified and automatic counts at a cordon line enclos-
ing the study area

(b) classified and automatic counts on screen lines inter-
secting the area

(c) home interviews

2.11 The data from these studies includes origin-destina-
tion, 16-hour classified counts (one day at cordon and
screen lines) and 7 day automatic traffic counter flows at
cordon and screen lines. Predictions from LUTS are monitored by regular update counts. This information augments
that assembled by ad hoc counts and other methods.

Economic evaluation

2.12 The D.Tp. computer program for the economic assessment of inter-urban road schemes (COBA) requires as standard input data, traffic flows assigned to the 'before' and
'after' networks. Traffic data are based on August 16-hour
daily flows coverted to annual flows making due allowance
for seasonal variation. Further data requirements include
M (the annual traffic multiplier), H (the percentage heavy
goods vehicles element in the August 16-hour flow), junction turning counts and accident rates for road links and
junctions.

Highway design

2.13 Technical Memorandum H6/74 recommends road layouts
and facilities appropriate to ranges of peak hourly and
average 16-hour daily flows. (ref. 2). The average daily
flow (summer peak) is used for primary assessment of rural
road schemes. Peak hourly flow is used for detailed
design with an assumed heavy commercial vehicle (HVC) content of 15%. To estimate peak hourly flow, a directional
classified traffic census is required on at least 5 three
day periods (Friday, Saturday, Sunday) during the period
June to August over 3 or 4 consecutive hours as appropriate
to include the one in which the highest flow is expected to
occur.

The average of the flows recorded in the same hour of the

me day of the week in each of the counts is calculated
d the highest average for any one hour is taken as the
ak hourly demand.

r urban roads, the peak hourly flow is taken for design
rposes.

nction design

14 For new roads, roundabouts are designed to carry the
aviest traffic flows predicted to occur in the design
ar. These flows usually occur at peak times but the
sign must also be checked for a combination of flows un-
r non-peak conditions.

r improvements to existing junctions, the design capacity
ould cater for existing flows scaled-up to allow for
owth and redistribution of traffic and should be compat-
le with the capacities of the approach roads.

.15 <u>Crawler lane</u> (rural roads) need is assessed by ref-
ence to average August daily flow and per cent HCVs.

.16 <u>Signal controlled intersections</u> The traffic flow
riteria for traffic signals at junctions are based on the
ur busiest hours in any 24 hours. This period is ident-
fied by classified turning counts usually between the
eriod 06.00 to 18.00 hours.

.17 <u>Pedestrian facilities</u> At junctions and elsewhere,
e type of pedestrian facility is determined by reference
volume and movements of both pedestrians and traffic.
enerally flows are measured over a 12-hour period, unless
e peak exceeds the 12-hour average by more than 50%. In
e case of at-grade facilities (zebras and pelicans), the
ehicular criteria are expressed in terms of the average
umber of vehicles per hour averaged over 4 peak hours.

.18 <u>Pavement design</u>

r the purposes of pavement design the number of commer-
ial vehicles (unladen weight exceeding 1500 kg.) and their
xle loads are considered - the effect on the pavement of
ther lighter traffic being disregarded. For design pur-
oses, traffic is defined in terms of the cumulative equiv-
lent number of 8,200 kg. axle loads.

raffic information from automatic and classified traffic
ounts enables an estimate to be made of the traffic at the
ime of construction, expressed in commercial vehicles per
ay (either in each direction or the sum in both directions)

and of a growth rate for calculating future traffic loading.

Estimates of annual flows of commercial vehicles, based on average daily flows assessed by short classified counts are suspect and compound the possible error inherent in the estimation of pavement life.

2.19 Traffic noise estimation

Calculations to determine the eligibility of residential property for compensation or insulation under the Noise Insulation Regulations are based on the L_{10}(18 hour) noise index. (Ref. 3). This requires the prediction of the traffic flow during the period 06.00 - 24.00 hours on a normal working day in the base year and the maximum which will occur within 15 years of the works first opening to traffic, on each section of any road which will contribute noise to each facade of the property, including the various parts of any junction. Predictions of the percentage HGVs within the flows and the mean vehicle speeds in these years are also required.

2.20 Traffic management

The role of traffic management as a method of optimising the capacity of highway networks has increased in relative terms in a period of severe financial constraints.

Traffic studies leading to the design of traffic management solutions call for:-

   (i) measurement of peak hour average 5-day and maximum flows (directional)

  (ii) 16-hour (06.00 - 16.00 hr.) average 7-day and maximum flows

 (iii) junction turning movements (peak hours)

  (iv) accident rates at links and nodes

   (v) seasonal and annual growth factors

2.21 Highway maintenance

The report of the Committee on Highway Maintenance (Marshall) recommended that highway authorities should keep sufficient records of annual average traffic flows on all their roads using sampling techniques wherever possible, so as to be able to determine reliably the average usage of the whole of their network by categories of road. Full coverage of all roads as recommended by Marshall is impracticable on resource grounds, particularly in the case of Class 3 and

unclassified roads and most counties limit their census
points to cover trunk, principal and the more important non-
principal roads.

2.22 Maintenance programmes

The preparation of programmes for structural maintenance requirements calls for the estimates of the annual average
daily flow of commercial vehicles and data are generally obtained from the multi-point countywide traffic census, by
automatic counts augmented by ad hoc classified counts to
identify the HCV element.

2.23 Surface dressing

The volume of traffic carried by a road is a major determinant in the selection of a specification for surface dressing.
For the design of surface dressings, traffic is considered
in terms of the number of commercial vehicles a day in the
lane under consideration, and an estimate of the appropriate
lane traffic category is made by ad hoc manual classified
counts, supplementing the information available from the
multi-point county census.

2.24 Accident studies

In carrying out their responsibility to promote road safety
in accordance with section 8 of the Road Traffic Act, 1974,
counties refer to the results of detailed analysis of road
accidents. The accident rate on road links is expressed in
terms of personal injury accidents per million vehicle-km.
and this calculation calls for the measurement of average
daily traffic flows (vehicles) in August.

2.25 Development control

Applications for planning approval to development need to be
assessed in terms of their traffic implications. Estimates
of the traffic generated by proposed development are derived
from traffic studies of existing development having similar
characteristics.

In the case of residential development, automatic traffic
counters sited on the access roads provide a method of quant-
ifying total traffic generation and the trip rates derived
from this and "home interview" data can be stratified by
socio-economic characteristics for use as a guide elsewhere.

The computer data bank of trip rates assembed by the County
Surveyors' Society and up-dated annually by national sample
surveys provides a point of reference for development control

studies and can also be used to assess changes in trip rates over a period of years.

3. METHODS OF ASSEMBLING TRAFFIC DATA

3.1 The results from a questionnaire survey of 15 of the 39 "shire" counties in England showed that an average of 33 automatic counters of the punch tape output type per county were used regularly in local traffic censuses. The maximum number of automatic counters reported was 80 and the least 13.

3.2 In six metropolitan counties a sample of four reported an average of 40 automatic counters (range 75-24). The number of counters used was roughly proportional to the population of the county.

3.3 From these statistics it is possible to estimate the total number of automatic traffic counters currently in use by the 45 metropolitan and shire counties in England at about 1500; this figure excludes the GLC, London boroughs and the district councils (met. and non met.). The total number of automatic counters in use for local traffic studies in the whole of England must be well in excess of 2000, and the capital value of the equipment at replacement value about £1.2-M.

3.4 All the shire and metropolitan counties responding to the questionnaire reported the use of temporary staff for the assembly of classified traffic data. Most expressed concern about the accuracy of the results and preferred trained enumerators for important ad hoc counts.

3.5 Another recurring problem arises from the traffic hazards of laying pneumatic tube detectors on the busier traffic routes (overcome by increasing use of inductance loops).

Vandalism to counters was also reported - few counties insure this type of equipment.

3.6 The methods adopted by counties for the storage and retrieval of traffic data vary and currently only about 20% of counties undertake storage and analysis by computer.

Some counties are seeking to introduce relatively sophisticated computer programs which link traffic and accident data and calculate accident rates.

4. RESOURCE IMPLICATIONS

4.1 Two shire counties with populations of 600,000

(50 counters) and 1,450,000 (32 counters) reported annual expenditure of £25,000 and £19,000 respectively in assembling traffic data by automatic means.

These costs include an allowance for depreciation of equipment, installation charges, maintenance, staff travelling and subsistence, and punch tape transcription. Taking the lower of these two costs, the estimated annual cost of assembling local traffic data by automatic means for the 45 English metropolitan and shire counties, but excluding GLC is nearly £0.9-M.

4.2 Manual counting is labour intensive and costly but is currently the only method of collecting classified traffic data. For this reason, total cost of assembling local traffic data exceeds by a wide margin the figure of £0.9-M. attributable to automatic data collection.

4.3 No figures are available for the costs of traffic data analysis, but they are clearly considerable in view of the quantity of data assembled and the variety of the outputs required.

5. CONCLUSIONS

5.1 The traffic data requirements of local authorities are extensive and a significant element of local resources for transport can be attributed to data assembly and analysis.

5.2 The need for a comprehensive base of traffic data for all aspects of highway design is recognised by local authorities but the scale of the problem and its financial implications emphasise the need for a higher degree of co-operation with the Department of Transport.

The scope for such co-ordination should be examined by the Department of Transport's Working Party on Traffic Data Collection which is currently reviewing the five systems of counting organised on a countrywide basis.

5.3 Ideally, national traffic censuses and the monitoring for the regional highways traffic model should form the framework upon which counties can superimpose local studies so as to provide traffic estimates on trunk, principal and the more important non-principal roads.

REFERENCES

1. Research on Road Traffic. HMSO, London, 1965, 23.
2. Technical Memorandum on Design Flows for Motorways and Rural All-purpose Roads (Technical Memorandum H6/74)

Department of the Environment, August, 1974.
3.   Noise Insulation Regulations, S.I. No. 1763,
      HMSO, London 1975.

5. Problems of present data collection and analysis

G. Penrice, CB, BSc(Econ), FRSS
Department of Transport

SYNOPSIS. The quality of manual enumeration is variable,
as illustrated by controlled experiments at three traffic
counting sites. Reasons for discrepancies are discussed.
The quality of automatic data collection may lead to
improved accuracy, particularly since longer traffic counts
are possible, although automatic equipment does not yet
provide a suitable classification by vehicle type required
for most purposes. Some of the limitations of automatic
data collection are summarised. Sampling in time leads to
errors in estimates of traffic flow over periods of interest
and an indication of accuracy levels for annual flow is
given. A particular difficulty with manual censuses is
that counting extensively during darkness or public holidays
is costly and impracticable. Sampling in space is
necessary in order to study traffic over a road network.
The variations in flow between different points is very
large and a large sample is needed to provide the required
breakdowns. Data processing problems are of great importance; the possibility, through automation, of increased
amounts of data will make good vetting procedures even more
vital. Some standardisation of data formats used by
different agencies would enable more data sharing and lead
to economies. The required accuracy of traffic data is
difficult to specify generally, but an indication is given
of tolerable levels of recording error. It may be preferable to concentrate more effort on improving the quality of
data and our knowledge of the errors rather than increasing
the quantity of data. Data other than traffic flow are of
increasing importance (eg speeds, following distances, axle
weights) and there is a growing need to measure these
variables more regularly.

INTRODUCTION

1.1 Traffic flow data collection is still on the whole
manually orientated. Where automatic methods of counting
are used they are almost entirely limited to unclassified
counts of all motor vehicles. Until now manual counts
have been essential in order to provide figures by types of
motor vehicle and pedal cycles. Equipment that will
provide counts by types of vehicle is being developed but
has not passed beyond the trial stage. This paper therefore concentrates on the problems of manual enumeration and
unclassified automatic traffic counting with an emphasis on
statistical implications and discusses how far the problems
might be affected by technological developments.

THE QUALITY OF MANUAL ENUMERATION

2.1 As with any other manual task an important factor is
human error. It is clearly helpful to know something about
the characteristics of this error and, if possible, to
quantify it. Unfortunately, only limited information is
available with which to assess the accuracy of manual counting. Automatic counts have also been taken at a number of
the Department's manual sites but at best a comparison can
be made only for total motor vehicles and any assessment
would be influenced by the errors involved in the automatic
counts.

2.2 During 1977 some counts were carried out simultaneously
at three sites by both a dedicated full-time team and by
teams locally recruited. All three sites were on single
carriage-way principal roads in built-up areas but in
different counties. The counts took place in spring or
summer so almost all of the eight 16-hour counting periods
were in daylight.

2.3 Compared with the dedicated team the results of the
recruited enumerators showed differences at each site, for
each day and for each class of vehicle. However, there
was considerable variation in the size of the differences
and there was no consistent overall bias either positively
or negatively: for total motor vehicles the differences in
the daily totals ranged from -6% (compared with the
dedicated team) to +6½%. There were very few cases where
exact agreement was achieved for any day for any individual
class of vehicle and there was a wide range of percentage
differences in the counts. For example at one site the
recruited enumerators on one day fell short of the dedicated team's count of light vans (under 1½ tons) by 78

vehicles or 21%. At another site on another day their
count of over 1½ ton 2-axled goods vehicles exceeded that
of the dedicated team by 42 or 19%. For cars and taxis,
differences ranged from -7% (-951 vehicles) to +5% (+559
vehicles). Even pedal cycles, which are easily distinguish
able, showed some high percentage differences, including
one of -16% (-36 cycles). The differences at individual
sites on a particular day are therefore serious both in
absolute and percentage terms. It is not known whether
the sites concerned in this limited test were typical or
whether the performance of the average enumerator is better
or worse than this.

2.4 There are several reasons why such discrepancies can
occur. If enumerators are recruited on an ad hoc basis,
there will be great variability between the quality of the
best and the poorest. In conditions of heavy flow, the
inexperienced may not be able to cope, and vehicles are
either missed or partially filled in by guesswork; the
correct vehicle classification may also be at risk in these
circumstances. Where counting is conducted from a caravan
or hut on one side of a road vehicles on the far side maybe
obscured and missed, or wrongly classified. Most counts
are run on a shift basis and continuity can sometimes be
difficult at the change of shift time. For hourly breakdowns of the data, accuracy depends upon enumerators' alert-
ness to the beginning of each hour and the reliability of
their wristwatches. There is of course no guarantee that
all enumerators will be conscientious all of the time and
counting teams are occasionally discovered not to be "on
the job". But the main problem for the one who requires
and commissions the collection of traffic flow data is that
he seldom knows whether the counting team is dedicated, inexperienced or careless.

THE QUALITY OF AUTOMATIC DATA COLLECTION

3.1 The use of any efficient traffic counting equipment
will avoid most of the errors described above, although the
pneumatic tube may sometimes record only one vehicle of a
pair that cross it simultaneously. The two main practical
differences between manual and automatic counting are that

   i. Automatic counting can be carried out for longer
       continuous periods for the same cost.

  ii. Manual counts until now have been the only
       established method of measuring flow by type of
       vehicle.

The need for classified traffic data is considerable, covering such major topics as vehicle-specific road accident rates per mile travelled and despite the undoubted advantages of the automatic counter, the inability to classify vehicles is the largest single weakness of the technique as at present operated.

3.2 The pneumatic tube detector, which has been the main-stay of many traffic counting authorities for a generation, has two serious weaknesses. First, on heavily used roads they quickly become lacerated and unserviceable. Secondly, they count axles rather than vehicles, which brings about inaccuracies even in the estimate of total flow, especially on roads where there is a high or constantly changing proportion of multi-axled lorries. Inductive loops do not suffer from either of these objections but on the other hand they do not have the advantages of portability. Loops which can be rolled on to the road surface at short notice are now available but they cannot be removed and reused. Another weakness of the inductive loop is that lane-straddling vehicles may be missed unless complex systems are employed.

3.3 A different question is that of mechanical failure. Of course as technology improves the chances of failure are reduced but, even with the best equipment, breakdowns or imperfect running will occur on occasions. When this does happen the consequences can be serious. For example, a temporary failure in power supplies would lead to a temporary break in recording, and careful scrutiny of data output is always necessary to check for the possibility of such time-slip error. Another problem is that with manual retrieval and interrogation a complete stoppage might be discovered only after several days or even weeks.

SAMPLING IN TIME

4.1 Apart from the truly continuous automatic count, all traffic censuses are measuring a sample in time of the total traffic flow on a particular stretch of road. They can be repeated every week, month or year etc, or they may be a once-off operation, sometimes for less than a day. From any of these relatively short counts it is usually required to estimate by scaling factors the flow in some longer period. The sort of factors that would be required are from a portion of a day to a day, from a day or days to a week, and from a week to an average annual week.

4.2 The statistical problem is how to decide on the appropriate monitoring site or sites from which to calculate the factors. Every site has its own hourly, daily and seasonal flow patterns and any combination of sites used to match the flow variation at the site to be scaled is likely to lead to an error of estimation. To obtain the seasonal factor, one of several approaches is to categorise sites into a few classes using a separate formula for each; another is to apply multiple regression analysis to derive a formula with several independent variables representing eg the percentage of commuter traffic, the percentage of weekend pleasure traffic and the percentage of evening pleasure traffic. Using the best methods available so far, the 95% confidence limits of annual flow estimators for use with 2 day manual counts can be narrowed to between $\pm$ 10% and $\pm$ 20% (taking all error sources into consideration) depending on the timing of the sample counts. Other less sophisticated but more widely used methods can sometimes produce errors in excess of $\pm$ 30%.

4.3 A particular problem of non-continuous censuses, and especially affecting manual counting, is how to estimate the traffic on public holidays and on the days surrounding them when conditions are abnormal. It is not easy to engage enumerators at these times and, even where it is practicable the cost is prohibitive when required on a national scale. Similarly, there are cost effectiveness considerations for manual censuses in respect of counting through the night, although accurate traffic data here can be of importance, for example in the level of heavy goods traffic or any vehicle class in relation to the number of road accidents. No satisfactory solution to these deficiencies can be achieved until equipment is readily available with a reliable vehicle classifying capability and which is preferably portable.

SAMPLING IN SPACE

5.1 When data collection sites are meant to be representative of a complete road network, we need a random (unbiased) sample in space of all the traffic levels in the network for the particular time of the count. Even when an efficient random sampling system is used the variability in flow is often so great that large errors are possible in the mean flows. For example, in a recent large scale benchmark census throughout Great Britain with an average of ten sites per road class per region, the 95% confidence limits of about a third of the regional road class total flow means

were in excess of $\pm$ 30% of the mean.   The errors for most
individual vehicle classes would have been even larger.

5.2 The only way to overcome this type of difficulty is to
count at more sites, but cost benefit considerations are
crucial here since the accuracy of sample means improves
only in proportion to the square root of the number of sites
It would appear that in the long run classified automatic
counting would be substantially less expensive than manual
counting, so it should be possible to improve efficiency of
regular sample censuses in this way at no extra cost with
the added advantage of extra accuracy enabled by a longer
time coverage.

DATA PROCESSING PROBLEMS

6.1 As with all data collection, some checks must be made
before any processing or tabulation is carried out.   The
main errors that could arise with either manual or automatic traffic data are incorrect or missing recordings, and
the possibility of transcription errors for manual data.
Data validation checks by the computer after input are
difficult to design without the production of a large error
output, which has to be scrutinised clerically.   On
inspection many of these apparent errors of recording will
turn out to be acceptable in respect of particular
conditions at particular counting sites.   To avoid transcription errors, and also to speed up data input, optical
mark reading census forms have been designed but the
Department's experience with these to date has not been
wholly satisfactory.

6.2 With any increase in the amount and variety of traffic
data obtained by automatic methods the need for efficient
methods of data vetting would become even more vital.   It
is possible to program into the validation procedures
certain logical tests, and these tests can be improved when
a history of data collection at a particular site is avail
able and checks can therefore be made by comparing present
data with those for previous time periods.   However, it
will not always be possible to exclude extreme values in a
logical fashion and an appreciable amount of subjective
assessment can never be avoided.

6.3 Many different authorities and agencies, including
Central and Local Government, are involved in traffic
counting in some form or another and it would clearly make
for economies if some of the data collected could be shared.
It is important therefore that the maximum amount of

standardisation is achieved both in the vehicle class and
road class categorisation used and also in the methods of
data capture. At present, data are available in a wide
variety of forms such as handwritten tabulations, printed
paper tape, punched cards, punched paper tape and magnetic
tape, and exchange of data is very costly and time consuming

THE REQUIRED ACCURACY OF TRAFFIC DATA

7.1 It is clear from the preceding discussion that there
are a multitude of sources of inaccuracy which contribute
towards errors in final applications of traffic data.
Recording errors are only one of these sources and even if
those errors can be reduced in the raw data, cost-benefit
considerations may dictate that it is not worth spending
too much on further improving the accuracy of recording
techniques, since the effect of such improvements on final
results may be very small in comparison with the magnitude
of other types of error.   On the other hand, it may be
beneficial to investigate very closely the actual recording
errors of existing equipment and to facilitate the
detection of such errors, even at the expense of reducing
the amount of counting.

7.2 The specification of minimum accuracy levels of
recording equipment is a complex problem due to the variety
of applications and due to the other components of error
involved.   However, as a rough indication of such
accuracy levels required in raw traffic count data, it is
considered that errors of ± 2% or more in only 5% of
straight daily flow totals would be satisfactory for most
purposes.   Provided the counting method is not biased (to
an unknown degree) this would imply an accuracy of the
order of ± 10% or better, with 95% confidence, for individual
hourly totals.   From the evidence on manual counting errors
in Section 2 this would probably represent a considerable
improvement over present practice.   For the classification
of vehicles, if 90 to 95% of vehicles were correctly allocated, this again would probably represent a considerable
step forward.

DATA OTHER THAN TRAFFIC FLOW

8.1 As mentioned in earlier papers, a number of types of
traffic data, other than traffic flow and its related
parameters, are assuming increasing importance.   These
include vehicle spot speeds, following distances, axle
loads and total loads, and weather conditions such as air
temperature, visability and road surface wetness.   The

technical facility for measuring and recording several of these items automatically already exists and work is being carried out to perfect recording methods for the remainder. The requirement now is for the setting up of a system of strategic monitoring stations whereby these parameters could be recorded and the data called up both on a regular and an ad hoc basis.

CONCLUSIONS

9.1 It will be apparent that there are a multitude of problems with the present data collection system, some of which might be resolved by technological developments.

9.2 However, there are two main points of caution to bear in mind. Firstly, such technological developments would increase the amount of data, which may impose considerable demands for retrieval, analysis and storage if full benefits are to be realised. Secondly, automatic recording would not eliminate all the sources of error, particularly those due to sampling in space and to sampling in time where direct measurements at particular sites are impossible or too costly.

Discussion on Papers 4 and 5

Mr Penrice (Paper 5)

The reliability of data must always be examined before any attempt is made to base conclusions on them. Manual enumeration has sizeable observer-variability in daily traffic counts, but the errors seem less horrific after allowing for the number of days covered and the variability of traffic flows; flows at individual points often increase seasonally by three to four-fold.

Vetting the accuracy of data is often unduly neglected, but there is the danger of over-vetting. Vetting procedures that were sensible when introduced have sometimes been carried on mechanically, resulting in series which were worse than those unvetted. There is also the danger of being too over-sold on linked data; their errors often accumulate rather than cancel out.

The difficulty in getting support for collecting sufficient data is not limited to the transport field. Even when only a small increase in the efficiency in the allocation or use of resources would justify a substantial increase in expenditure on information.

A substantial shift towards automatic counting is now desirable. Paper 9 suggests that even at this early stage of development, automatic counting provides main categories with a similar order of accuracy as manual counts. The Department of Transport spends about £800,000 a year on manual counting and on the 200 point census could probably recoup the costs of going mainly automatic within about three years. In information rich systems attention becomes the key design variable. This has implications for analysis, the clear presentation of data and puts the impact on decision takers. Also the actual counters may be working well but can users in practice get the results in the form required? Often with difficulty.

Discussion on Papers 4 and 5

Mr M.S. Bourner (Kent County Council)

As a transportation engineer I am very much concerned with the use of traffic data to help solve particular problems. Over recent years analysis techniques have become more and more sophisticated and this sophistication has led to the gradual change in requirements for data bases. Often, however, the need for substantial quantities of different data precedes the ability to collect it in a cost effective manner. One area where this has been highlighted in recent years is in the need to separate traffic flow into its directional components on two-way roads.

Detailed analysis of directional traffic flows can reveal some interesting facts. For example, Fig. 2.1 shows flow information for a monitoring point on the outskirts of Maidstone and reveals that the predominant flow during the evening peak is in the same direction as the morning peak which is perhaps a little unexpected from a superficial glance at the total flow pattern

Collection of directional traffic data has been essentially a manual exercise with automatic devices being employed only occasionally where there is good lane discipline. Many instances occur, however, where lane discipline cannot be guaranteed, as shown in Fig. 2.1. In 1965, the Park and Ride experiment in Maidstone triggered off the development of a new type of portable equipment to give directional traffic data cheaply at almost any desired site. The equipment uses a pair of sensors laid across the whole carriageway as shown in Fig. 2.2. At present conventional pneumatic road tubes are used and the necessary logic has been built into a standard Golden River traffic counter. Table 2.1 shows some of the applications where directional flow information is advantageous or even essential.

With increasing costs of manual data collection, I am convinced that we are on the threshold of a substantial increase in the use of automated devices to do this job for us. However the project in Kent has demonstrated that machines must be designed to meet the needs of the engineer rather than forcing the engineer to use whatever data a machine produces. The opportunity is at hand to do great things with automation, and this opportunity should be seized, with the machines working for us and not vice versa.

One thing I have found is that it is almost universally true that as one mentions statistics to the public they switch off and one's arguments are lost for ever. We in Kent County Council are attempting to get over this problem by the use of television. We bought a simple monochrome system for general survey work. We found that we could make reasonably accep-

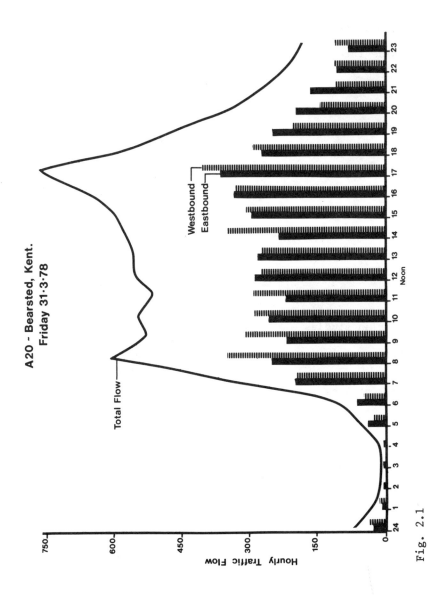

Fig. 2.1

TABLE 2.1 *Uses of directional flow information*

Roadside interview surveys — provides management information during the preparation stage enabling correct staffing levels to be planned for each survey point

— provides back-up information on traffic flow during the interview period

— provides longer term information on variation of flow at survey point

Registration no. surveys — as for roadside interview surveys

Car park studies — provides information on arrival and departure rates and car park occupancy

Pedestrian studies — helps in routing analysis

Public transport studies — provides information on passenger loadings

Network studies — comparison of 'modelled' and observed flows by direction highlights assignment or matrix errors particularly for peak hour models

Flexitime studies — by using directional flow information associated with major traffic generators, network loading models can be constructed to simulate the effects of flexitime on peak period traffic flow

Junction design — provides necessary details of entry and exit flows on each arm of a junction

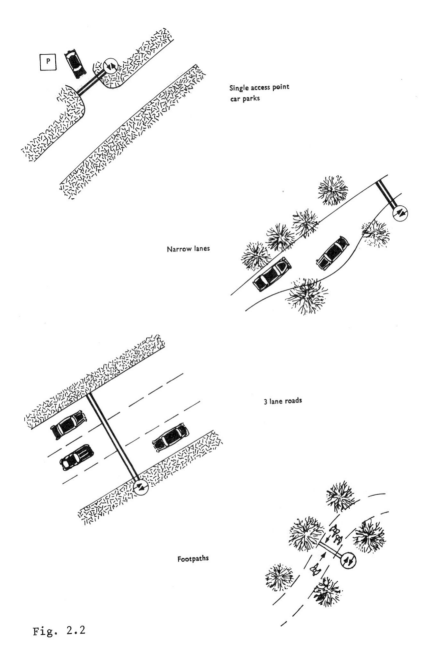

Single access point
car parks

Narrow lanes

3 lane roads

Footpaths

Fig. 2.2

Discussion on Papers 4 and 5

table films with a little extra expenditure on the necessary
studio equipment. This technique of putting information on
film and by translating it into scenes that the general public see with their own eyes has a profound effect. For
example, the conventional way of portraying the problems of
congestion is to put a map up and draw lines to show queues
but many people do not understand maps, and this form of diagram means absolutely nothing to them. As an alternative,
we showed on film queues forming, extending back and finally
disappearing from sight at well known locations. Very few
figures were quoted, but the information was there in a form
that the public understood.

In this conference the use of TV as a method of collecting
link data has not been widely explored. Kent County Council
have been doing some experiments in this field, particularly
on the problem of turning movement counts at junctions.
Using video tape, we film traffic movements mainly at peak
periods and then select only the information we are interested in for the analysis in hand. Traffic data captured in
this way is most useful because different observers can go
back to the film and pick off different information at different times. One person may be interested in cyclists,
another in pedestrians, and yet another in heavy vehicle
movements, and so on. With data on film there is no need for
total immediate analysis for storing in digital form.
Although a much improved method of data collection, it is
however still basically a manual method. Investigations into
automating data collection from videotape has revealed that
it is possible to interlink a high speed computer and video
frame store. Some experiments with such equipment have shown
that it is possible to identify a wide variety of vehicle
movements and classify vehicle types completely, automatically and cheaply (on a marginal cost basis). Unfortunately the initial cost of the equipment at present is
rather high.

Mr M.J. Hampton (Essex County Council)

Sample counting (one week per month is suggested) seems to be
of value. In Essex, the lack of sufficient loop sites makes
this impractical at present as, with the frequency of sampling the sensors must be in place permanently, with the
equipment brought to each site at intervals as required.

This approach may be worthy of consideration by the Department of Transport in its proposals for re-organizing the
national census.

72

Mr J.A. Bailey (GEC-Elliot Ltd)

Regarding expenditure, the amount of money being spent on data collection represents only ½% of the proposed expenditure on roads.

Mr I. Corsie (Norfolk County Council)

The specific needs of the Department of Transport for traffic data have been separated from those of local authorities. Although separate its two needs are inter dependant and the data requirements of each are bound to overlap. It would be a good thing if the conference demonstrates a framework within which both local and central government can collect data without duplication but to proper standards of accuracy.

Mr J. Hammond (Department of Transport)

With devices which are capable of collecting so much information there is danger of getting too much and then not really knowing what should be done with it. This is not the case with maintenance, where there is a dearth of relevant traffic information available to the engineer. He needs to know about total flow and the proportion of heavy vehciles as well as about other things such as expenditure and road condition if he is to decide the standard of maintenance he should adopt. Total flow is necessary to assess the benefit to the community of keeping a road in operation and heavy vehicles which do the damage to the roads largely determine the cost of applying a particular standard. Taken together total flow and heavy vehicle flow should indicate the economic standard of maintenance.

Obviously, the ideal way of getting this data is by a continuous method, but we have to be selective about how we get the information. Unless a specific count is mounted we can only estimate the flows in a given situation. It is clear that we cannot afford enough sampling points to support reliable traffic estimates at all points in the network, but great accuracy is not necessary. This was established two or three years ago when the Association of County Councils, in a Working Party under Peter Deavin, investigated the maintenance of minor rural roads. They came to the conclusion that it was very much more difficult to do traffic counts on little used roads, but again it is not important to be accurate as long as the field of accuracy is defined.

It is probably sufficient to know that the total flow on a particular road lies within a particular flow band with a proportion of heavy vehicles within an expected range for that band. If roads could be grouped in this way from existing

or proposed sampling points each flow band could have an
associated standard of maintenance relevant to its traffic
characteristics. Proposals for grouping roads in this way
have been made by the Standing Committee on Highway Maintenance and if found to be acceptable by county surveyors will
considerably simplify the need for traffic data for maintenance purposes.

Mr Mathews (Paper 9)

Management of traffic data for adequate quality at the right
price is really the nub of the data collection problem. It
is largely a problem of making sure that the data collected
is what is required to the required standards and that it is
stored in a way such that it can be readily retrieved. Data
costs money but it does not of itself provide any extra road
space or save any lives. However much data is collected, it
will never be sufficient to remove all uncertainty. Decisions will have to be made supported by insufficient and
often rather uncertain information. Thus, the data and the
data collection resources need to be used in the best possible way. The operation needs to be controlled and managed
better, treating it almost as an industrial process and pay-
ing attention to aspects such as quality control.

Some people believe that just because they have an estimate
which is more accurate than another, this is necessarily good.
Obviously, this depends on whether the greater accuracy is
really necessary in relation to the decisions to be made and
how much is being paid for that accuracy. There are many
cases where the quality of information required for the decision is quite coarse and the expenditure to collect the data
need not be large.

Counting with automatic equipment poses a problem because
there is inherently less flexibility available. A reasonable
duration of count is needed to ensure that valid data are
being produced. Despite the trend for the greater use of
inductive-loop detectors, there are many sites with moderate
to low traffic flows where pneumatic detectors should suf-
fice, even for continuous counting, and the additional investment to install a loop system is not essential. If one has
as part of the management system, information on the types
of faults occuring at each counting site, it is possible to
take corrective action which might even be to install loop
detectors in place of a pneumatic tube. It is worth remem-
bering that the proportion of multi-axled vehicles on the less
busy roads is usually quite small and thus the over-count
from a pneumatic detector is also small and can be neglected.

The work in Kent of time-dependent variability has been
mentioned. Parallel to this, work is in progress at TRRL to
attempt to model the variations of traffic flow in terms of
time-dependent variations in occurence of different trip purposes. With the help of a statistical consultant, the
results are beginning to show promise. One difficulty in
such a study is that on most of the roads which are of real
practical interest, there is a mixture of trip purposes.

Mr L.B. Yates (GLC)

We in the Greater London Council have about 90 counters and
we have about half of those installed in permanent locations.
This accounts for 28 points. So we are fairly active in the
automatic counter field. There are two teams operating in
two separate vans to look after all of these counters and
they install new counters at ad hoc points as well as vetting
those at permanent points. About half of the 28 permanent
stations are looped. We feel that better accuracy is
obtained when there are loops, and there is a lot less danger
when servicing these particular positions.

It is unfortunate that the reduction in staff has coincided
with the mass arrival of our data, and as a consequence we
are lumbered with a large vetting problem. This is a problem
because vetting out all the extreme differences probably
means vetting out the variation that you are trying to record.
It is not always easy to make a judgement of what is an
extreme flow and what is wrong.

In addition to the automatic traffic counters we carry out
manually classified counts on our series of cordons and screen
lines. The automatic traffic counters are permanently
installed but the manual sample counts are carried out on
two, three or four year cycles.

There is a great need for more interchange of data between
authorities and this certainly applies in London. Sometimes
two authorities record the same data.

Data may not create roads or save lives but it does enable
one to use resources more efficiently and I think it does
help one to save lives by identifying problem points and
doing something about them.

Mr M.F. Hardy (Hertfordshire County Council)

Herts County Council spend around £30,000 a year just on
traffic data collection, which allows us to collect on some
230 sites on the links on the main road network. One of the
main reasons for the difficulties at the present time, particularly among senior people is because we have not thought

about the issues and problems that are going to be arising
in the next five or ten years. If these problems and data
requirements that are going to help analyse those problems
and produce solutions are not considered, I think we are
going to continue to find that we are in the position we are
in today, namely having a lack of information. It is very
important to think about the form, presentation and use of
the data.

One of the things that interests me is how complex information can be put across in such a way that it really is
understood and it can be taken account of when those in responsible positions have to take decisions? Hertford County
Council did a lot of work in the late 1960s and early 1970s,
with fairly crude flow diagrams and overload diagrams which
are now improving in the accuracy of the information and in
the presentation. It is not just a question of overload on
roads. Members are now very interested in environmental
issues and accident situations. Data has to be brought
together on those three aspects and presented in a way which
puts over the total picture at the same time. This helps
members in decisions on levels of investment and on priorities. When looking at trends however over a span of a very
few years one has to have very accurate data to get anything
that is reliable.

If a site is deteriorating it is important to know if it
is getting rapidly worse or if it can be put up with for
another year or two. Regarding monitoring a much more positive system is required, where the design engineer, whether
handling traffic management or road works, catalogues
exactly what he expects to happen in terms of traffic flows,
accidents, noise, and so on, and that it is properly recorded
so that after the event, the forecasts can be compared with
the actual events. It is a much better discipline for the
design engineer not only to think about the job he is concerned with but the implications in all the surrounding dis-
tricts and surrounding roads.

Mr H.J. Langton (Haringay)

Simple counts of traffic moving along links is a comparatively
small part of the total amount of traffic data collection
which we are involved in as an urban authority. Junction
counts are a very important part of our work which also includes O and D surveys with number plates, home interviews,
road-side interviews, and so on.

The work also involves a lot of counts on pedestrians,
particularly on pedestrian routes rather than just actual
movements across a road. This is difficult because people

resent being stopped if they are on foot and asked where they
are coming from and where they are going to. Parking surveys
are still done on the street by people with clipboards.
Sophisticated equipment seems to break-down on roads
where traffic is congested and where lane discipline is non-
existant. All of this is expensive and involves the use of
temporary staff on a large scale, which is fraught with difficulty. Manufacturers seem to be in a race now to develop
even better equipment along the same lines, and what many
urban authorities need is a different type of equipment altogether. Time lapse photography is a technique we have used
and attempts have been made to develop automatic pedestrian
counters using photo-electric cells. This is the sort of
equipment I would like to see manufacturers developing. It
could be simple to use and could be used as an every-day tool
in the same way that traffic counters are.

Mr B.C.W. Jennings (Department of Transport)

One of the difficulties that the Devon Sub-Unit face is that
the case to be made for a given level of provision is often
a marginal one. As a result we came to the conclusion that
automatic data collection was an essential pre-requisite to
a full understanding of our traffic problems. Data has been
collected from about 1969 to date and one interesting aspect
of this information is how stable with time the distribution
of flow throughout the year is for specific links in our network. The counters used originally on trunk roads were of
the manually read type and these were later replaced by fully
automatic counters.
The manual counters and some of the older automatic counters are now being employed on side roads to provide additional information for junction design and to broaden the
general data base.
On the subject of accuracy, difficulty has been experienced
with tube counters where flows approach 30,000 vehicles per
day. We are moving over to the newer type of loop detector
in the hope of improving accuracy and reliability, but by
and large we reckon that the multi-axle effect on the counters we have been using is compensated by under-counting
during peak periods.
Data from the counters is checked several times but one of
the more important checks is that done by the project team.
It is essential that the people who are directly involved
with projects should vet the data themselves and be sure
that it is sound, because sooner or later they are the people
who have to defend any decision, be it to a committee or to
the public.

Discussion on Papers 4 and 5

   The Department of Transport has embarked on an open
approach and problems of communication with the general public are likely to be greater than with Council Committees.
It is not always easy to simplify issues such that they may
be readily understood by people who have no traffic enineer-
ing expertise. Perhaps the challenge lies here.

Mr A. Christie (TRRL)

Even if automatic classification is introduced on a large
scale there will still have to be many manual counts for
special purposes, eg for the monitoring of lorry controls,
information is needed which cannot be collected by automatic
means. The most common lorry control affects vehicles over
three tons unladen weight. These can only be recognized from
the reflectorized plates which they carry at the rear.
   Could some of the inaccuracies of manual counts which have
been mentioned be due to difficulties caused by rather large
number of vehicle classes usually employed? In studying the
effects of lorry controls accurate classification is necessary and ways of improving it have been considered. Firstly
it seems essential to reduce the number of vehicle classes
adopted to the minimum necessary for the particular study.
Secondly, manual tallies should be avoided: there is a danger
that they will not be reset at the end of each hour and, if
there are many buttons, the wrong one may be pressed. The
final and main requirement is adequate staff control, ie
selection, training and supervision. Without these pre-
cautions substantial errors certainly do occur.

Mr R. Moore (TRRL)

In his Paper Mr Fry indicated that his working group had
recommended a rather radical move towards automatic vehicle
count and classification techniques and that a computer
based data base, including road links, might be employed.
He has further indicated that 200 permanent sites would be
employed, with the addition of a rotating census at a number
of temporary sites. Is his working group convinced that the
increased cost of analysis and data storage justified all
200 points being permanent? Should there perhaps be only 50
or so permanent sites and the balance of data from the remaining sites collected on a sampling basis? The existing 200
point data is currently collected on a sample basis.
   Mr Searle's Paper emphasized the need for continuing an
enhanced collection of axle weight data. The Transport and
Road Research Laboratory operates 4 permanent and 8 sampling
sites on motorway and principal roads, and it is possible

that with additional funding, this could be expanded in the future. Individual vehicle data has been collected by the Laboratory on a sample basis from the M4 motorway in September last year. Only eight hours of this particular data was collected, but it included vehicle class, speed, inter-vehicle gap, individual axle weight, total vehicle weight, each axle space dimension and total vehicle length for two lanes out of a three lane motorway. Similar data is currently being collected on the M6 Midlands link.

Dr Wood suggested that if vehicles were run over weigh-bridges at slow speeds some of the dynamic compared to static weight problem could be overcome. The measure of dynamic axle weight is a product of a large number of variables and factors. The road profile for perhaps a third of a mile prior to the actual weighbridge is very important. Then there is the vehicle suspension system and the tyre pressure. Vehicle speed is a factor but a relatively small one. Unless vehicles were brought down to crawling speeds a dynamic to static weight factor will be present. At crawl-ing speeds the problem of vehicles braking or accelerating on the weighbridges would produce an additional dynamic fac-tor.

The Laboratory will be installing automatic classification equipment at six 50 point and 200 point sites this year. These will be evaluated over a year to find out what sort of data losses occur, equipment failure, the cost of data analy-sis, how much data patching is needed and to develop methods of data patching for this much more complex collection of data. Some of this data will be fed to the data users to find out if it really is the data that they want, and if the data is in a form for suitable analysis.

Dr J. Shaoul (University of Salford)

I am surprised about the restriction of the use of traffic data to the road links as opposed to including juctions as well, since nearly ¾ of the accidents in urban areas are at junctions. With respect to both congestion and safety, by restricting oneself to the performance of the highways as measured by links, one is leaving out a lot.

On the question of evaluating the system with respect to the road links, the kind of data that is being suggested might usefully be collected also leaves room for considera-tion and discussion. There has to be guidelings as to how one can evaluate the performance of the highway system, which after all, is concerned with moving objects on the road. What has to be evaluated, has to be specified and

then machines that will collect the necessary data have to
be designed, or alternative methods of collecting this information have to be specified so that the best data will be
obtained.

Evaluation of highways requires that the effect on the
driver's behaviour of road narrowing or road widening,
gradients, road widths, number of lanes, road structures
and furniture such as central reservations, traffic islands,
bollards, road markings etc. be known. The effect of different traffic flows within these different situations have
to be known. Thus, data relating to driver behaviour for
each of the different road configurations and ranges of
traffic densities are required. This entails sampling the
different road conditions at different times.

When talking about assessing highway performance in terms
of behaviour, this involves relationships between road users.
This means that the manoeuvres carried out by drivers, both
with respect to the road and other road users, the distance
between road users, the relationship between road users
(passing, following, crossing, approaching, lane changing,
leading etc) and their position, speeds as well as flows in
each direction, should be known.

There is also the question of other road users, particularly pedestrians who are part of the highway system and cannot be ignored. A pedestrian may precipitate an accident by
his action, although not himself be hit by a car. Consequently, pedestrians must also be included in any such evaluation of highway performance, assessed in terms of roaduser
behaviour.

Dr J. Tough (Wootton, Jeffreys and Partners)

Regarding the use of television, this is being employed by
the Police both to put over messages to the public and as a
training technique. For the traffic engineer both film and
video recording usefully enhance manual classified and
turning movement counting.

I have been involved in research aimed at semi-automating
the abstraction of data from video recordings and similar
work is being carried out using aerial photographs. With a
semi-automatic system, although vehicle coordinates must be
transcribed manually, this can be done by unskilled staff.
The rest of the process, the interpretation of the transcribed data, is carried out automatically, enabling the
measurement of any parameter which depends upon the spatial
and/or temporal positions of vehicles.

Work is also being carried out to automate fully the
transcription of video traffic data. A video signal is a

series of analogue images of a scene at precise intervals of time. Complex pattern recognition procedures are necessary to interpret video signals and determine vehicle positions.

Difficulty is experienced with some automatic traffic count analysis programs because, their indication of faulty data is unrealistic. It is possible to get so many flags indicating faulty data that they are not worth looking at. The software houses must ensure that their programs give reliable data fault indications which the engineer knows he must take notice of. This is a difficult problem requiring a sophisticated solution but it has been solved in the ATC analysis package supplied by Wootton, Jeffreys and Partners. It is a great help to the traffic engineer if faulty ATC data can be identified in as meaningful a way as possible.

Mr H. Palca (Department of Transport)

In Mr Fry's working group we started off with the idea of a smaller permanent core of 100 sites, allied to a three-monthly rotating set of 4 cores, also of 100 sites each, with only 2 of the 4 cores being used again in the succeeding three-monthly period. However when this hybrid scheme was tested, we found that the variance of the estimate of traffic changes from one quarterly period to the next was unacceptably large. It therefore seemed preferable to widen the geographical coverage of the rotating sample by changing all its sites in successive time periods, and to increase the number of sites in the permanent core. No permanent core can adequately cover all the different varieties of roads; 50 to 100 sites are clearly too few, and 200 sites are likely to be the minimum needed to ensure that at least the main types of traffic patterns and densities are adequately represented for continuous monitoring of national traffic trends.

Mr Jones (Paper 4)

The comments of Messrs Hardy, Corsie, Bourner and others underline the importance placed by Local Authorities on the establishment of a sound framework of traffic data to assist in the quantification and solution of the wide variety of problems they face.

Mr Corsie touched on one of the main policy issues to emerge from the conference, namely the necessity for a greater degree of compatibility between the traffic data assembled by the Department of Transport and the Local Authorities. It is only by greater co-operation that this

objective will be fulfilled. As things stand, the two principal agencies involved in traffic data collection approach
the problem unilaterally, and this is wasteful in the use of
scarce resources and valuable equipment.

The Terms of Reference of Standing Traffic Data Liaison
Committees (STDLC) set up in connection with the Regional
Highway Traffic Model Project might usefully be extended to
cover the urgent requirement for the production of a specification for the assembly of traffic data by the Department of
Transport and Local Authorities, and for arrangements to be
made for sharing the compatible traffic data assembled in
this way.

6. Current automatic traffic counting practice

P.M. Gater, BEng, and R.K. Duley, CEng, MIERE
Sarasota Engineering Co. Ltd.

SYNOPSIS. This paper examines some of the principles of
modern traffic counting equipment practice. Both traffic
sensors and data recording techniques are reviewed together
with their appropriateness to differing situations. The two
main groups of traffic sensor axle detectors and vehicle
detectors are described. Particular emphasis is placed on
the inductive loop vehicle detector and the pneumatic tube
as both are widely used. Details are given of various
inductive loop configurations which can be employed to
optimise counting accuracy. Data retrieval aspects are
treated by a comparison of two basic types of system. These
are directly read records, such as electromechanical
counters or printed tape, and machine readable records such
as punched tape or magnetic tape.

1. INTRODUCTION.

Originally traffic counting was performed by employing
people to stand at the side of the road with notebooks and
record the number of vehicles passing within a given period
of time. Nowadays the high operating costs of manual
counting and ready availibility of automatic traffic
counters has resulted in most authorities using automatic
equipment wherever possible. Nevertheless in applications
where it is required to study the composition of traffic by
counting vehicles in groups, according to type, or where
particular turning movements are of interest, manual
counting is still used.

An automatic traffic counting installation needs to be
equipped with vehicle detectors and a means of recording
the data. According to need these may be housed in a
portable instrument case if the installation is temporary or

in a roadside cabinet if it is permanent. Data can be recorded continuously on a simple electromagnetic counter or accumulated over timed intervals and output on a printer or in a machine readable form such as punched tape or magnetic tape.

In addition to simple volume counting equipment is available which will classify vehicles into groups according to length and speed of travel and record the number in each group separately. New developments are likely to make available equipment capable of classification by vehicle type together with measurement of speed and headways.

2. VEHICLE DETECTORS

For its vehicle detection equipment, automatic traffic counting owes much to the development of vehicle actuated traffic light control systems. This is because in the late 1920's it became necessary to improve junction efficiency by making the controllers responsive to the flow of traffic and not just dependant on a fixed timer. Hence a vehicle detector had to be developed which would operate reliably for long periods without attention.

The first detectors to find wide application were pressure sensitive types. These are mounted in the road surface so as to be operated by the pressure of the wheels of the vehicles as they pass over. Early pressure sensitive detectors used the principle of two metal plates, acting as electrical contacts, which were brought together when the pressure was applied, but reliability problems lead to the introduction of a pneumatic device.

Eventually, ever increasing traffic flows resulted in unacceptable short lifetimes from even the pneumatic types despite their being mounted in elaborate steel frames. In consequence alternative techniques, which did not require mechanical contact with the vehicle, were sought. Of the many which have been tried the inductive loop detector has become the most widely accepted. In these detectors the presence of the metal body of a vehicle is sensed by virtue of its effect on the magnetic properties of a loop of wire buried in the surface of the road.

2.1. Pressure sensitive axle detectors.

In modern automatic traffic counting the pneumatic detector has been adapted for use in temporary sites. The sensor consists of a stout rubber tube approximately 12mm in diameter which is secured to the road surface by means of

special nails. One end is partially sealed and the other is
connected to an air pressure sensitive switch in the
traffic counter so that pressure applied to any part of the
tube by the wheel of a vehicle is detected. The
installation can be performed rapidly with minimum
disruption to traffic.

As an alternative to the pneumatic detector there are
available pressure sensitive devices in which the air tube
is replaced by a piece of coaxial cable, such as is used
for television aerial feeders. These operate on the
principal that pressure on the cable causes a small voltage
to be developed between the core and screen of the cable,
which can be detected by a suitable amplification circuit.
This type of detector features a much faster response time
than pneumatics and it is claimed that the durability is
better.

Whilst the short installation time required for the pressure
sensitive axle detectors is very attractive for temporary
sites the vulnerability of an exposed surface mounted sensor
renders them unsatisfactory for a more permanent
installation. A further disadvantage is that axle detection
gives only an approximation of the number of vehicles
passing as different types of vehicles have different
numbers of axles. In consideration of this, most traffic
recorders can be set to divide the number of input pulses
by two when axle detectors are connected.

2.2. Inductive loop vehicle detectors.

By virtue of being buried in the road surface inductive
loops are not susceptible to wear and tear by passing
traffic. Even when they do fail this is usually
characterised by a complete cessation of counting, which is
readily identifiable, whereas pneumatic detectors tend to
give a period of distorted counts prior to a failure. In
addition loop detectors can be set up to give a single
output for most vehicles, regardless of the number of axles,
hence high counting accuracies can be achieved.

Traffic counting systems utilise rectangular loops typically
1.5 metres in the direction of traffic flow and between
1 metre and 3 metres wide depending on the width of road to
be covered. A loop consists of two or three turns of wire
with the free ends twisted together to form a feeder to the
detector at the roadside. The wire is laid in slots cut
typically 5 to 7 mm wide by 30 to 50 mm deep, by means of an
abrasive saw, and backfilled with molten bitumen and/or an

epoxy resin compound.

The most effective placement of loops for traffic counting has been the subject of considerable research. Much of the original work was done in the 1960's by the then Ministry of Transport, arising out of the need for continuous accurate information on traffic flows for the development of area traffic control systems in the "West London Experiment" (See ref.1)

2.2.1. <u>Single lane counting</u>. Where a traffic count is required from one lane only a single loop connected to a single detector is required.

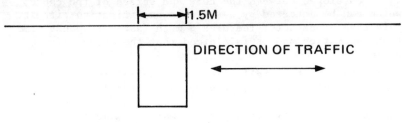

Recommended dimensions are given in the appropriate graph in appendix 1.

2.2.2. <u>Multi-lane counting</u>. When the counting site includes two or more lanes it is not sufficient just to extend the detector loops across all lanes. The reason for this can be seen by considering two vehicles in separate lanes. If the second vehicle moves over one part of the loop before the first vehicle has left its part of the loop only one continuous output will be given. This would lead to severe undercounting.

Recommended dimensions are given in the appropriate graph in appendix 1.

Where lane discipline is good the easiest remedy is to install a separate loop and detector for each lane and feed the detector outputs via a "Serialiser" to the traffic recorder. The serialiser ensures that if a vehicle arrives over each of the lane loops at the same moment, the simultaneous outputs from the detectors will be converted into the appropriate number of pulses for recording.

2.2.3. "N-plus counting". When good lane discipline cannot be guaranteed at a counting site, errors will be caused by vehicles which straddle two lanes thereby operating two detectors and being counted twice. This can be largely overcome by using the N-plus system, so called because it incorporates more loops than "N", the number of lanes available. Ideally the loops should be arranged such that :

a) The widest vehicle does not straddle more than two loops.
b) The narrowest vehicle does not pass between any two loops.
c) Two vehicles side by side must cross at least three loops.

The outputs from the detectors are then fed to a "Counting Logic" module which will give outputs under the following conditions for a 2 lane, 3 loop layout :

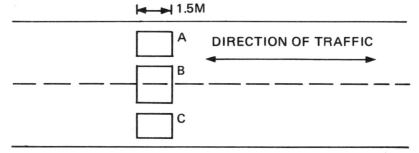

Recommended dimensions are given in the appropriate graph in appendix 1.

Operation of A or B or C produces one count immediately.

Operation of A and C together or A and B and C together produces one count immediately and a second count after a short delay.

It is seen that operation of single loops or adjacent pairs A and B, or B and C produces only one count, but operation of A and C together produces the first count followed by a second count a short time later.

The 3 lane 4 loop system works as follows :

·Recommended dimensions are given in the appropriate graph in appendix 1.

Operation of A or B or C or D produces one count immediately.

Operation of A and B and C or B and C and D or A and D produces one count immediately and second count after a short delay.

Operation of all four loops produces one count immediately followed by a second count after a short delay, followed by a third count after a further short delay.

2.2.4. <u>Directional systems</u>. All systems so far described, whilst normally used to count vehicles travelling in a single direction, are equally responsive to vehicles passing in both directions. By using two loops, two detectors and a "Directional Logic" it is possible to obtain separate signals according to the direction of passage.

A typical layout for a single lane is shown below. The way in which the loops are overlapped is chosen to minimise interference between the detectors.

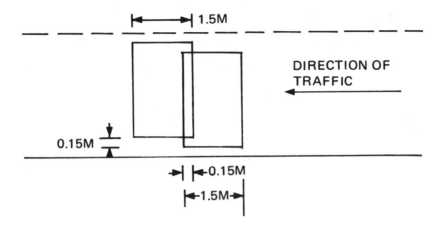

On multi-lane roads where there is no central reservation to separate the traffic a directional pair of loops can be installed in just the offside lane to help eliminate errors caused by overtaking vehicles in the oncoming direction. This is termed a "unidirectional" or "U/D" facility.

Two examples of loop placement for counting systems with U/D are shown in the diagrams below.

ONE LOOP PER LANE DIRECTION OF TRAFFIC

DIRECTION OF TRAFFIC

89

"N PLUS" LOOPS

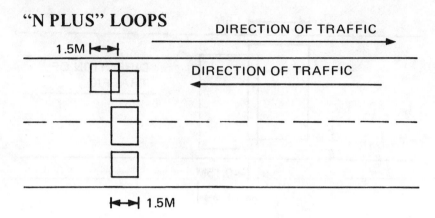

-3. TRAFFIC DATA RECORDERS.

Instruments for recording traffic counts are required to work in very adverse environments. This is particularly true if they are used at temporary sites without the benefit of a protective roadside cabinet. In consequence they are frequently supplied in weather resistant cases which can be padlocked to a suitable post at the roadside. Many recorders also include an integral sensor for axle counting or a loop detector.

3.1. Simple recorders.

The most simple type of recording technique is the electromagnetic counter. These increment each time a count input is given and the data is accessed by visiting the site periodically to read the total number of counts which is displayed through a window on the unit.

3.2. Time based recorders.

Often it is required to count the number of vehicles during different periods of the day. In this case a recorder is needed which will count and record the number of vehicles in equal time intervals, typically every hour, in such a way that the data can be accessed and interpreted readily. The record is usually in the form of printed tape, punched paper tape or magnetic tape cassette, although some units with solid state memories have been developed.

A printed record is the most immediate way of accessing

data as it can be read directly without the need for any
additional equipment. If, however, significant amounts of
data are to be collected and it is intended to process this
by means of computer equipment a machine readable medium
such as punched paper tape or magnetic tape is to be
preferred. This avoids the time consuming and error prone
task of entering the data manually. *

Data can be processed on many types of computer equipment
such as micro-processors, mini computers, time sharing
systems, programmable calculators etc. In most cases,
however, it is necessary to use an additional "translator-
unit" to convert the records into a form compatible with
the input required by the computer. The advice of the
recorder manufacturer should always be sought in this
area.

Of great importance in the function of a time based
recorder is the master clock for if this fails to operate
accurately the data can become distorted. The most modern
recorders now use quartz crystals, similar to those used in
electronic watches, in this function. Provision is usually
made for the selection of the recording time interval to
allow for very detailed studies over short periods or
conservation of the recording medium for long term
operation.

4. COUNTING SYSTEM INSTALLATION.

Most traffic authorities need traffic data for a variety of
purposes. This involves the collection of data at fixed
sites on a continuous or intermittent basis together with
temporary surveys at sites of transient interest.

4.1. Temporary sites.

The requirement for a temporary counting site can arise in
many ways, typical situations are as follows :

(i)   Counts for accident studies.
(ii) Traffic flows from local events.
(iii) Peak hour traffic flows.
(iv) Support data for planning appeals and public enquiries.
(v)   Before and after studies on road improvement projects.

Portable weatherproof equipment is normally used in these
circumstances utilising a pressure sensitive axle detector.

* Some recorders offer printed & machine readable records.

Nevertheless, some authorities do prefer to use inductive loops and this can be achieved by using metallic adhesive tape on the surface of the road. This technique was pioneered by London Borough of Camden (See ref.2).

4.2. Fixed sites for periodic counting.

Periodic counting at fixed sites is usually carried out to obtain data samples for statistical purposes such as computing average daily flows. Such sites are usually equipped with permanent detector loops and the recording equipment is installed when data is required.

Some periodic sites provide little more than a connection for portable equipment whilst others are equipped with road-side cabinets containing shelves on which equipment can be placed. The latter practice is to be preferred as it has been found that the equipment is less subject to deterioration. This is because the cabinets are usually heated to prevent condensation, have no exposed connections and are generally less susceptible to casual damage.

In some instances it can be advantageous to equip periodic sites with permanent detectors and electromagnetic counters and just use the time based recording periodically.

4.3. Fixed sites for continuous counting.

Continuous counting is employed where it is necessary to monitor factors such as growth and seasonal variation of traffic flow. The data from such sites may prompt further investigation at other types of sites. In almost every situation detectors and recorders are installed in roadside cabinets or huts.

REFERENCES.
1. HAM R. Area traffic control in West London. 2 vehicle counting detectors. Traffic Engineering & Control, 11 (4) 1969, August, 172-176.

2. HODGKINSON D. REINKE B. The development of a new traffic counting system. Traffic Engineering & Control, 15 (14) 1974, June, 648-651.

3. RATCLIFFE B. MACKIE D. Focus on handling traffic data. Traffic Engineering & Control, 16 (1) 1975, January 15-19.

4. TRAFFIC COUNTING. Publication of Sarasota Engineering Co. Ltd.

APPENDIX 1A   **LOOP WIDTHS—ONE LOOP/LANE**

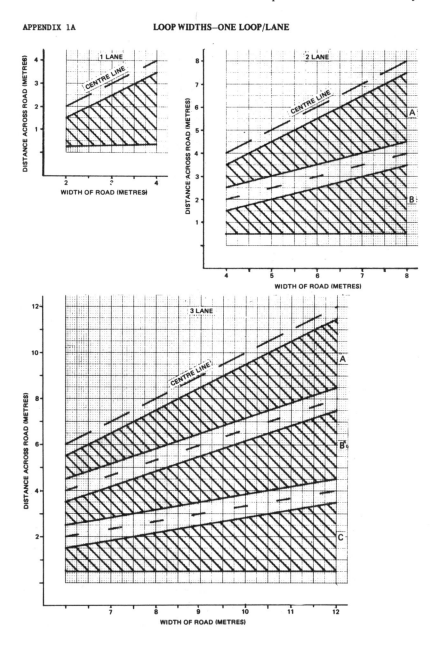

APPENDIX 1B   "N PLUS" LOOPS

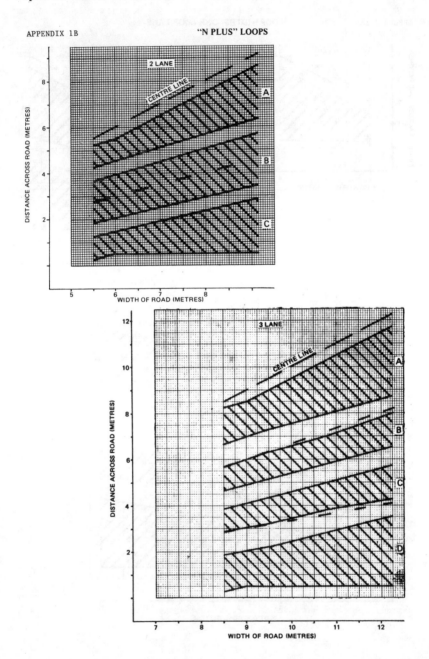

7. The installation of instruments

G. Kent
G.K. Instruments Ltd.

INTRODUCTION

It is the intention of the Author of this paper to review the current practice in the application, installation and maintenance of both portable and permanent sites for the acquisition of traffic data. It has long been felt that the equipment that has been available has been adequate for the collection of data in a simple form, but that instrumentation has been relegated to the bottom of the league in its importance by the users and when required to function, has been found to be wanting for the lack of care and simple maintenance.

Similarly, the installation of such instruments, be they portable or permanent, in many cases leaves a lot to be desired, and that attention to small detail is the difference between good and bad results or in some cases, no results at all, and that in general the facilities afforded to traffic instrumentation in the form of workshop, test equipment and a few tools and training should be reviewed if the maximum amount of return in the form of good data for the investment is to be realised.

With the advent of instrumentation enabling not only volumetric counts but speed, headway and vehicle classification, it is imperative that more thought be given to the way in which government and local authorities view the acquisition of data.

Basic care of instruments

1. That upon receipt of instruments, the intended operators should read and digest the operating

instructions and ascertain the basic capabilities of the
equipment in their possession. So often the damage is
done first and then reference is made to the instruction
manual.

2. That in lieu of any basic maintenance, a high order
of cleanliness be observed, then this will go a long way
to eliminating problems at a later date, so often we see
traffic recorders as a haven for small insects, through
supposedly sealed cases. It has been known for one ear-
wig in the wrong place and the wrong time to bring a
recorder to a halt!

3. That personnel involved in the operation and maintenance of traffic recording data, should be allowed to
attend a training course with the relevant manufacturer
where a simple schooling in the appreciation of instrumentation could be given, together with a course in the
basic operation and maintenance of equipment and its
application.

4. It should be possible to achieve a 10 - 15 year life
expectancy or even longer with our own company's products
and yet so often we see instruments in appalling condition
after 2 - 3 years, this situation could be very simply
reversed with just a modicum of care and attention.

Installation of portable sites

It is estimated that 95% of all traffic data collected is
obtained by the use of portable equipment, i.e. pneumatic
tube coupled to a pressure sensitive switch inside a portable traffic recorder, the whole being padlocked to a
convenient post. Improvement in the use of this, the
simplest form of data collection, can be made in the
following ways:-

1. Attention to the hardware used in the fixing of the
road tube, the present method of clamps and nails is so
often badly installed that within hours a section of the
installation is adrift; however, a well laid tube using
plugs to accept the road nails will provide a more
positive fixing. It should be made known that this
system of axle detection has remained unchanged in 25
years and that the only deviation from this has been the
introduction of the flexible 'chinese finger'.

2. The introduction of the electronic air switch introduced to the United Kingdom 4 years ago has done much to

improve the state of the art, eliminating the need for adjustment and when used in conjunction with a sealed road tube, i.e. a nail in the other end of the tube, the ingress of foreign matter to the diaphragm is negligible and that the addition of this switch alone will do much to improve the accuracy of axle detection.

3. The provision of a paving stone in rural sites at the point of installation of the recorder will do much to reduce the introduction of foreign bodies and water etc. during inspection visits, or better still the use of a low cost cabinet will do much to improve reliability and provide a first line of protection and also help to prolong the life of the equipment.

4. As an alternative to the pneumatic tube, the intro- duction of a 'cable sensor' a small diameter, stainless steel coaxial cable that generates a signal when pressure is applied from an axle, and is capable of outlasting the pneumatic tube by a factor of 10, the cable being taped to the road for short town counts and set in an adhesive for semi permanent applications.

The cable is then connected to a transducer capable of being used with most manufacturers equipment in place of the diaphragm or electronic air switch. In view of the fast electronic response time of a million times faster than a pneumatic tube, the chances of coincidental pulses in multilane traffic are reduced to a minimum. The econo- mics of using this system are as yet unknown but look as though they will be favourable in cost with the pneumatic hose together with the accessories required and the labour involved in installing the conventional system.

5. The need for a rigid check out procedure upon visiting site, an example of an inspection can be seen in the Trans- port and Road Research Laboratory bulletin 9. Adherence to the use of such a procedure will again do much to elim- inate the most obvious point that wasn't checked at the time of the visit.

Semi-permanent sites

As an alternative to the road tube, we, as a company, have been instrumental in the introduction of the semi-permanent site comprising of a permanent loop installation, the loop tails being terminated in a simple lockable post mounted box, containing a programmable socket. When a traffic

'A typical semi-permanent installation'

'Recorder loop input plug'

'Press detector reset button, and detectors automatically tune'

'Recorder closed and secured'

count is required, a recorder containing detectors and logic is taken to site and plugged in, the socked programming the logic as to the number of loops in use and whether the installation is an 'N' or 'N+' configuration. It remains then only for the operator to switch the recorder on and note the pertinent details of the site, the start time and date to set the equipment in operation.

Such a system has been employed by Northamptonshire County Council, where over 40 of the semi-permanent sites have been installed, they being of the two loop configuration, the sites strategically placed in positions where vehicle lane discipline is extremely good. The result being that a directional count is available at all the sites. An estimate of the cost of such an installation for both the loops and the installation of a post mounted socked is under £100. Installation for such a site being accomplished at the rate of two a day.

With regard to the economics of such installations, a site used on a 3 month rotational basis would pay for itself in a year, against the laying of the conventional road tube each time a count was required. In addition, the measure of confidence in the installation will rise and the need for weekly visits to site to check the installation will be reduced to a level at which the recorder demands checking. Similarly, the safety of personnel is greatly enhanced by the lack of need to inspect the primary element.

As a point of interest, the cost of a 2 channel recorder used on this system, with two self tuning detectors to give a directional count is approximately £700. The output tape being an 8 track ASC11 coded computer compatible tape capable of being read at speeds of up to 500 cps, such a tape containing a month of hourly directional data could be read into a computer in 20 seconds, alternatively input via a 10 cps teletype terminal would take 15 minutes.

Permanent sites

1. For some years, permanent counting stations have steadily been installed throughout the United Kingdom in an effort to produce long term trends. The majority of these installations having been equipped with mains power enabling reliable data to be collected over long unattended periods. While this collection of data can be accomplished by the use of semi-permanent site equip-

'Type 600 cabinet showing rack mounted instruments'

'Rear view of instruments showing input/output connectors'

ment, the use of a cabinet combined with mains power does much to provide a first line of defence against a hostile environment. Furthermore, with the advent of both 'ALICE' and micro-processor based systems, the ability to expand on existing sites must do much to reduce the overall cost of such installations. However, to accomplish this, it is essential that the initial work be of such a standard that expansion is possible. It is then imperative that the loop installation in the first instance be accurate to allow for the addition of a second loop together with an axle detector, when a site is to be expanded for speed or vehicle classification.

2. A typical installation based on the Department of Transport's Type 600 cabinet is shown opposite, the cabinet being fitted with a simple rack allowing the proposed instrumentation to be used at a particular site to be quickly slid into position, connection of the loop inputs power supply and recorder being obtained by the use of the appropriate plug or socket. In the particular case of the installation shown, the system based on the Sarasota 215 CM detector allows for two isolated outputs from each lane, one of which is fed to the recorder via the logic, for permanent count purposes, the other being available for use with analytical equipment, or alternatively, for use with a data retrieval system.

3. With regard to roadside cabinets, the choice available is governed by the material of construction, aluminium being by far the best material, but the durability coupled with the cost of fabrication being reflected in the price. The alternative is mild steel and providing adequate attention is given to the protective finish and care is taken to avoid damage during installation, good service can be obtained from a housing a third of the price, but for a shorter lifespan.

Workshop facilities

1. Anyone with any experience of data collection in the field will agree that the best organised personnel are liable to make basic mistakes when installing and commissioning instrumentation, in the hostile conditions that are so often experienced even here in the United Kingdom, and that even the simplest of tasks, like wiring a terminal block can take a long time and result in errors. It is, therefore, imperative that personnel be prepared before going to site and have reduced the amount of work to be

done on site to a minimum, therefore allowing ample time for checking the installation. To this end, proper workshop facilities should be provided together with good lighting and heating; provision too should be made in the way of benches and orderly storage facilities for spares and components. Of prime importance is the need to keep instrumentation clean, and the use of a vacuum cleaner will do much to maintain equipment in a pristine condition. Similarly, a small expenditure on the right type of tools enabling routine maintenance to be carried out should be made available.

2. With regard to test equipment, an "Avo" or a "multimeter" will be sufficient to measure voltage of batteries, current drain, and in general test circuits. This, together with a "Megger" for the testing of inductive loops in the first instance will remove a lot of doubt about equipment performance.

3. Provision of test gear in its simplest form again will do much to diagnose possible problems before the actual installation and these should take the following form:-

A. A pulse generator, capable of inputing pulses to a recorder, will serve as a check on input capability.

B. A digital clock on the wall will serve as a master time piece for all personnel involved and enable equipment to be time tested or set up for roadside use before going to site.

C. A model comprising of a series of inductive loops, similar to that used for demonstration purposes by detector manufacturers, which can be used to check on both detector and logic performances removing all doubt as to instrumentation condition.

The above equipment can be purchased or better still, constructed by the personnel involved and will lead to a greater understanding of what they are trying to achieve. The value of a check procedure taking only a few minutes, as a matter of routine, will do much to improve the quality of the final output data. The total expenditure on tools, instrumentation and test gear in the first instance could be purchased for a cost of around £200; a small price in view of the capital investment involved and the need for good reliable data.

Summary

To briefly summarise the situation, it is imperative that
more thought be given to the whole process of data
collection with a view to further improving the percentage
of good data available from census points. It is, therefore, time to review the status of data acquisition within
the appropriate authorities if the quality is to be
improved.

8. Data collection systems

D.G. Hornby, BSc, CEng, MIEE
Plessey Traffic Co. Ltd.

SYNOPSIS. The requirements for traffic data are many and varied. The paper describes how traffic data may be collected and used immediately to provide information to drivers or be simply gathered and used for longer term analysis. Temporary and permanent collection systems are covered including the various forms of transmitting the data to a common centre.

1. INFORMATION

Remote control and monitoring systems have been used for many years by the public utilities for the control of electricity, gas and water. Extensive use of highly complex systems has been demonstrated by the aerospace industry and during the last few years centralised control and monitoring of traffic flows has been growing with the introduction of Urban Traffic Control and Motorway Communication systems. Private cable networks, rented Post Office private telephone lines, the use of public switched networks and radio have all been used to effect the communication path between the central control office and the outstations in the network. In the majority of applications the outstation has not only been used to control switchgear, pumps, traffic signals etc, but also to monitor performance and gather data. The experience gained in overcoming the normal transmission problems of attenuation, noise and corruption can be applied to the remote gathering of data from roadside outstations. These outstations may be specially designed to monitor vehicle flow, density, occupancy, speed, length and other parameters necessary to provide the statistics for the justification of construction programmes, new transport policies and so on.

Described in this paper is a range of typical systems
currently in use to provide traffic data for a variety of
purposes. They indicate the degree of variety and
complexity available to potential users of such networks.

2. DATA COLLECTION IN TRAFFIC CONTROL SYSTEMS

2.1 Sydney Australia. Waterfall-Bulli Pass Freeway
                        surveillance

A Freeway covering some 40 kilometres between Waterfall and
Bulli Pass in Australia has been instrumented with traffic
control signals, Toll registration, Emergency telephones
and a traffic surveillance system.

This system installed in 1975 uses the same data trans-
mission message format as the Department of Transport
Motorway Communication system installed in the United
Kingdom, and the traffic surveillance equipment supplied to
Australia was designed to use that format.

The control is implemented by matrix indicators mounted on
mast arms over each carriageway. Each indicator is
remotely operated from a police control centre using a data
transmission system running the length of the motorway.
The indicator warns the motorist of hazards and displays
the appropriate speed restriction. The area is liable to
continuous periods of fog and poor visability and it is most
important in the interests of public safety that the drivers
respond to the indicated message.

The D.Tp. motorway data transmission system in the U.K.
(Ref.1) has the capability of returning complex traffic
data via the normal message structure. This surveillance
system is the only one of its type to make use of this
capability to transmit driver behaviour information back to
the control centre. It is interesting to note that a
number of detectors were installed on the U.K. M6 and M62
but made use of a separate data transmission system.

The police monitor the driver behaviour in terms of the
total traffic flow past each monitor point and the number
of vehicles exceeding a speed threshold. This may equal
the indicator speed displayed on the freeway or may be set
higher or lower by police action at the control centre.
Motorcycle patrols are dispatched to sites where speed is
excessive and offending motorists can be cautioned.

A pair of vehicle detector loops is installed in each
traffic lane close to an indicator. The loops are

connected to a pair of detectors having identical
performance which count and measure the speed of each
passing vehicle. Lane discipline is good and a pair of
loops per lane provides the required counting accuracy.
The detectors in turn feed a detector logic unit which
provides an interface with the data transmission system.
The logic unit contains a speed threshold register which is
remotely set from the control office. The threshold is
normally set to the indicator speed on view to the motorist
but can be addressed at any time by keyboard operation to a
higher or lower threshold. The logic unit will then count
all vehicles travelling above the threshold speed and will
also provide a total count of all vehicles in that traffic
lane. The speed thresholds can be set between 10 and
100Km/hr in steps of 10Km/hr.

There are twelve detector logic units in the freeway system
and these are interrogated by the central office computer
on a rountine five minute scan. In order not to lose data
due to this relatively low polling rate local storage is
provided at the outstations to count up to 510 vehicles and
up to 63 vehicles exceeding the set threshold speed. The
data collected is displayed on two VDUs, one for northbound
and one for southbound traffic. Each VDU displays the
indicator legend on view at each point, the traffic volume
in vehicles per hour for each traffic lane and the
percentage of vehicles travelling above the speed threshold.
An alarm condition related to the number of vehicles
exceeding the speed threshold is also displayed.

The complete system is self monitoring and any fault in the
data transmission, signal control, telephone or vehicle
detector equipment will be displayed on the VDUs.

The computer records the total volume of traffic at six
detector sites and prints out the 15 minute flows and the
daily totals for each site once every 24 hours. The flow
measuring sites are placed at freeway entry, exit and
interchange points so that changes in traffic trends can be
monitored.

2.2 Automatic data collection in Urban Traffic Control
    Schemes

A number of Urban traffic control schemes have now been
installed in towns and cities throughout the world. These
control the traffic by influencing the traffic signals in
the area to provide a co-ordinated flow for the prevailing
traffic conditions. Excluding abnormal perturbations the

traffic conditions normally vary depending on the time of
day and the day of the week. A manual traffic study of the
area is carried out before the system is commissioned and
the conditions for critical and non-critical periods are
documented. These may cover morning peak, evening peak and
off peak traffic for weekdays as well as special traffic
conditions at weekends. A traffic plan for each period is
generated and stored by a computer which controls each set
of traffic signals via a data transmission network.

The original study should provide plans which are near
optimum at the time of the study, but traffic conditions
will change and the plans will need revision from time to
time to accommodate the changed conditions. In a non-
adapting system this is carried out by operator instruction
using data collected from vehicle detectors to update the
stored plans, and monitor the effect of the revision.

The vehicle detector most commonly used is the inductive
loop type which by the addition of suitable logic is able
to register the formation of queues, road occupancy, the
density of traffic in vehicles per mile and by using pairs
of loops, the traffic speed.

To obtain an effective control system, the data required to
control the traffic signals needs to be transmitted at
intervals in the order of one second. With systems
installed in the United Kingdom, this is most commonly
accomplished by connecting intersection controllers to a
dedicated telephone line from the computer room. A 16 bit
control message is transmitted to each controller and a
reply message of equal length returned once per second. It
is often economic to use part of the reply message for the
detector data as the detectors and their processing logic
are usually sited in free flow conditions close to an
intersection and its associated data outstation.

The data transmission standards are well specified by the
Department of Transport and have been adequately described
elsewhere. (Ref.2).

The precise format of the reply message will depend on the
particular system configuration. For example, the City of
Nottingham installed an Urban Traffic Control scheme in
1975 with 35 detector sites to provide flow and occupancy
data.

Each site typically contains loop detectors and logic
equipment to provide flow and occupancy data in each

direction of traffic flow, and a standard data outstation
to transmit the data to the control centre. The flow data
is obtained from the conventional n + 1 detector system
with a small buffer store to hold the count data between
successive 1 second transmission to the control centre, and
2 data bits are used to transmit the most significant data.

Occupancy is achieved by digitally timing the duration that
vehicles occupy all loops in one direction of flow at that
site. Although a high time resolution of 5 msec. is used
additional logic is added to compress the data irrespective
of the number of lanes at the site such that only 5 data
bits are used to indicate 100% occupancy.

In addition detector fault monitoring logic is added to the
equipment covering each flow direction and 1 data bit is
allocated to this function.

A complete 16 bit reply word is shown in Fig.1.

This data is processed by the computer at the control
centre and used to provide the following information:-

(a) a tabular display on a VDU showing for each site
     during the AM and PM traffic peaks:-

     (i)   a cumulative total of vehicles from the
            start of the peak
     (ii)   the average rate of flow
     (iii) a moving average of the occupancy

(b) a continual monitor of each site for "higher
     occupancy", such a condition being brought out
     via a printer as a system alarm. Further flow
     information may then be obtained from the VDU.

(c) a continual periodic flow count which is stored
     in the disc backing store to provide a flow
     profile for each site. This information is then
     developed on to paper tape each month for
     comparative purposes.

The previous section describes how conventional urban
traffic control systems have the capability to collect
and process traffic data. Current active development into
self adaptive traffic control systems such as the S.C.0.0.T
(Split Cycle and Offset Optimisation Technique) project
being undertaken jointly by the Transport and Road Research
Laboratories; the Department of Transport and industry will
provide an enhanced capability because of the comparatively
large numbers of detectors such a technique demands.

Inbound Flow								Outbound Flow							
1	2	3	4	5	6	7	8	9	10	11	12	13	14	15	16

16 bit reply word

Bits 1 and 9	Detector Fault Monitor
Bits 2, 3 and 10, 11	Flow Count
Bits 4 to 8 and 12 to 16	Occupancy Count

Fig. 1. Typical Detector Site Reply Word
Used in a Standard U.T.C. System.

Fig. 2. The Portable Data Capture Unit.

2.3 Small scale control systems

It is of course, not necessary to consider large computer systems to effect traffic control measures. For example, in West Sussex a configuration of loop detectors and associated logic, to determine vehicle speed, has been installed in association with a special sign to indicate violation of the speed limit to passing motorists. (Ref.3).

Another example is a system installed near Ascot to measure vehicle headway and again a special sign is illuminated to indicate to passing motorists that they are travelling too close.

A further example is a system being installed in Clwyd to measure traffic queues and again, actuate a secret sign to warn motorists of the hazard ahead, normal visibility of the hazard is impaired by a hump-backed bridge.

3. DATA COLLECTION IN ANALYSIS SYSTEMS

Current technology equipment and systems covered in this section may be classified as transportable, portable and permanent.

3.1 Transportable systems

The advent of high technology electronics now enables portable/transportable equipment to economically perform an analysis function at the data collection site.

An example of this has been the recent work done by the Police Scientific Development Branch of the Home Office in collaboration with Sussex Police Authority. (Ref.4).

There was a need, at a number of temporary sites, to measure vehicle speed, length, headway or classification of vehicle type. As the sites were temporary a permanent power supply was not available and the equipment therefore utilised battery supplies. To achieve maximum battery life low power semi conductors (CMOS) were used in the logic together with a microprocessor. The microprocessor provided a powerful analysis and data reduction capability to enable the data derived from temporary "stick down" loop detectors to be stored for up to 5 days on a standard tape cassette. The whole equipment was mounted in a strong metal box.

Arrangements were made to replace batteries and cassettes within each 5 day period, the cassettes being taken to a central off-line data processing computer for further analysis, detailed print out and permanent record.

It will be appreciated that with unattended systems of this type high reliability and low vulnerability to external damage are prerequisite for their effective use. It would seem that the two system elements worthy of further detailed development are the temporary road surface sensor arrangements and the cassette recorder. Long life "stick down" sensors are required and by using the most technically advanced semi conductors, which can provide a static storage capability, the electromechnanical cassette recorder could be eliminated.

3.2 Portable System

It is recognised that there will be a continual need to carry out traffic surveys which use personal interpretation of events. Origin and destination surveys and the need for special manual count surveys are typical examples. Traditionally the "clip board" and pencil have provided the data recording method which in turn necessitate conversion into machine language form for subsequent analysis.

The system described below, although nothing to do with traffic, illustrates how modern technology can speed up and improve this man/machine interface.

A portable data collection equipment based on a micro-processor which is used to gather ordering information for a supermarket chain has been in use for at least four years and the latest version has been designed to be carried "shoulder-bag style". The inputs to the equipment are from a keyboard and "pen" using fibre optic techniques which reads a bar coded label.

A photograph of the equipment is shown in Fig. 2.

The shoulder unit houses rechargeable batteries, a cassette recorder and the electronics. The 16 key keyboard and data pen are part of the unit but can be hand held via extendable leads. Data entered via the keyboard may be checked using the decimal display prior to being recorded, data entered via the data pen being immediately recorded. Should there be an error in the bar code information from the data pen an audible alarm sounds and the input process is repeated. When the tape cassette becomes fully loaded during the input process an audible alarm will sound and a new cassette may be loaded.

It will be appreciated that with numerous supermarket branches throughout the country the objective is to centralise all the ordering information at a common distributing warehouse. This warehouse houses a central data collection computer system which is connected via the public switched network to each store. The recorded cassettes are loaded into a data transmitter in each store and transmission to the central computer commences during the night time cheap tarrif rates. Each store transmitter is actuated in turn by the central computer.

If transmission errors are detected by the computer receiver unit a signal can be transmitted to remotely rewind the cassette mechanism.

3.3 Permanent system

The need for a widespread (30 miles radius) data gathering scheme was identified as part of an experimental police traffic resource allocation system installed in early 1976. (Ref.4). To achieve an optimum economic and functional balance in transmitting the data to the central computer several methods were evaluated. The first of these was the use of the public switched network. This has the advantage that line transmission rates are only paid for during connection time but this cost reduction has to be balanced against the more complex terminal equipments required at each end of the line. An alternative using permanently rented lines was considered, this has the advantage of allowing lower cost terminal equipment but this is off set against the continual line rental charge.

In both cases the possibility of transmission errors being introduced by the particular link method was investigated.

It should be appreciated that the economic break point between the methods is totally dependent upon the functional requirements of the data collection system and the degree of errors that may be tolerated. Factors such as line distortion; interference, unobtainable numbers, wrong numbers, together with the local data storage capability and the frequency of interrogation from the central processor must be taken into account in the evaluation. It is also feasible to consider a hybrid or satellite approach whereby a distant outstation is connected to the computer by the switched network and is in turn connected to remote vehicle detector sites by rented private circuits.

This hybrid or satellite solution was in fact chosen in the

system referred to above. The central computer was
connected to a number of microprocessor based outstations
via the switched network. Each outstation was designed to
collect data from up to 8 pairs of loop detectors serving
8 traffic lanes. Four of these traffic lanes were usually
situated close to the outstation site, the remaining four
lanes could be several miles remote from the outstation.
The vehicle detectors at these remote sites were connected
to the outstations by tone generators and receivers over
rented lines. The raw detector-data was processed by the
microprocessor to produce speed, vehicle length, and inter
vehicle gap information. This information was stored
locally in semi conductor stores awaiting interrogation
over the public switched network by the central computer.

The overall system outline is shown in Fig. 3.

4. CONCLUSIONS

This paper has attempted to indicate a diversity of system
applications that have been implemented. It is evident
that there exists a capability based on many years of
experience to effect the gathering of data at centralised
or distributed centres. There appears to be every
indication that such systems are required but it would seem
that a set of defined user needs are necessary before
investment into hardware and software design should
commence. In the event that this idealistic approach takes
too long, it is suggested that limited operation trials be
instigated as a positive step, to more clearly define user
needs and test system concepts.

5. ACKNOWLEDGEMENTS

The author wishes to thank his colleagues in Plessey
Traffic for their contributions and the Plessey Co. Ltd.,
for permission to publish the paper.

6. REFERENCES

1. D.G. Hornby "Motorway Communication System"
   paper presented at VIth World Highway
   Conference in Montreal.

2. "Data Transmission" S.L.S. Barnes. Seminar
   at T.R.R.L. 21/22 April, 1971.

3. "Automatic Speed Signs on Evaluation" Dr. R.
   Eagle and Chief Inspector B.D. Homans. Police

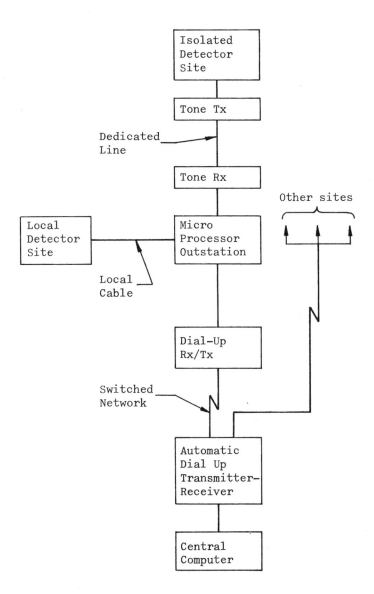

Fig. 3. System Schematic for Data Collection Network.

Research Bulletin. Vol. 78. 1976 p.9.

4. "Traffic Data Collection". J. Freer, Traffex
   1977 Seminar.

Discussion on Papers 6, 7 and 8

Mr Gater (Paper 6)

Automatic Traffic Counting is very dependent on the reliability of its sensors for long term accuracy. This is why the
inductive loop is generally used in preference to the pressure sensitive type of detector, unless the installation is
of a very temporary nature. Unfortunately with the rapid
spread in use of inductive loops there has been an increasing
number of situations where poor installation and management
of the loop and feeder has resulted in premature failure or
unnecessary damage by Public Works such as installation of
drains, water pipelines etc. This has caused some unfair
criticism of the inductive loop techniques.

For reliable installation the following are recommended.
Feeders should be run in ducts beneath the pavement and not
in slots in the road. Loops should be made of robust flexible wire buried at least 2 inches below the road surface and
reinforced with an epoxy resin. All joints should be sold-
ered and thoroughly waterproofed. The loop performance
should be checked before it is used. In order to achieve
this, adequate supervision of contractors is essential.

Recent figures from one of the counties who adopt this type
of standard for their traffic light installations show that
for a year's study over 316 loop sites with Sarasota detectors
the MTBF (mean time between failures) of loop plus electronics was in excess of eleven years. Our own records show that
the reliability of the electronics alone is in excess of 45
years MTBF.

For traffic classification a high standard of loop installation is mandatory. In this application it is usual to em-
ploy a basic configuration of two loops with 3 metres between
the leading edges. Vehicle speed can then be derived from
the time for a vehicle to travel the 3 metres and vehicle
length from the time to traverse the known length of the sec-

Discussion on Papers 6, 7 and 8

ond loop. It can be seen that errors in the geometry of the
loops will result directly in classification errors.

Mr L.B. Yates (GLC)

Rubber tubes have been in use for about twenty years, and it
is about time that something better was thought of for short
period counts. To install a rubber tube is a very dangerous
and hazardous operation.

There is also the problem of a tube breaking. If it breaks
at five o'clock on a Friday night, with no chance of maintenance until Monday, there is 3 inches of tube flapping around,
which could very easily get in the wheel of a motor cycle or
bicycle, with unfortunate consequences.

The GLC have tried using a material called Bituthene for
the temporary installation of tubes; it is self-adhesive and
is very quickly stuck to the road. It comes in long rolls
and one can cut it into strips, about 6" x 1½". Instead of
squatting in the road, banging in a nail, it is stamped on
and the tube is fixed. There are problems. It does not
stick very well in wet weather, nor when it is very cold -
but it is at least quicker and safer.

There does not seem to have been any serious consideration
regarding the replacement of the rubber tube. We will always
want a count for one to three days, and a loop installation
or anything that entails cutting slots in the road is no
answer.

Mr Kent's figure of under £100 seems very cheap for a loop
installation.

Mr Kent (Paper 7)

We at G.K. Instruments can cut two sites a day. The cost
for this is a minimum charge of £100. If we can do two sites
the approximate cost is £50 for the loops for each site. The
expensive part is not the loops but in getting to the site
and physically getting started. Most loop sites can go in for
around that sort of figure. That allows for another £40-50
for installation of the post and commissioning the site.

Mr J. Hillier (TRRL)

I understand headway is strictly a matter of time. It derived from trains and adapted in traffic terms it is now regarded as time headway or distance headway. When talking
about gaps it is distance or time between the front and back
of vehicles. The gap must be related to the front vehicle.

118

Mr K. Sriskandan (Department of Transport)

For the purpose of determining a distributed load that is
equivalent to traffic loading on bridges, the headway measurement that is required is the distance between the rear axle
of one vehicle and the front axle of the next.

Mr D.L. Swale (Traffic Technology Limited)

With transducers one gets what one pays for. The problem of
costs here is that the market is a small one, and no signifi-
cantly large quantities are involved.
  We in Traffic Technology Ltd thought that vehicle detectors
could be used in the traffic signal control field and that
this would provide the bread and butter basis for the rather
better quality transducer that may be needed for analytical
purposes. But they seem to be diverging rather rapidly, in
the sense that an analyser is a very demanding application
and demands a high quality output in terms of the actual
pulse used. It is difficult to reconcile this very small
quantity with this demanding specification and arrive at an
acceptable cost.
  The tribo-electric detector, which Traffic Technology Ltd
manufacture was developed a little more than ten years ago
as a result of collaboration between industry and the Transport and Road Research Laboratory. It is not by any means a
new device and there are many hundreds in service at the
ent.
  It is also worth mentioning about axle detectors, that
they have a different function and, essentially, the axle
detector is a passage detector whereas the loop is capable
of detecting a static piece of metal - a stationary vehicle.
They are regarded as complementary. In the traffic analyser
systems we manufacture we use both types of detectors.

The Chairman

It is worth bearing in mind that transportation interests
may have been expanded tenfold in ten years, and few countries
have actively or adequately investigated their traffic date
base needs.

Mr M. Gedda (VBB, Sweden)

In Sweden there is a road network which is the responsibility
of the Swedish road administration, except in urban areas
where roads are maintained by the local authorities.
Local authorities spend approximately 1.0-1.3* Skr per in-

---

* £1 = 8.465 Skr

habitant per city on traffic counting. Studies regarding
systems for automated traffic counting, have been carried
out by VBB during 1975-1977, commissioned by the Swedish
traffic research delegation and the national road authority.
The primary objective was to test the possibility of reducing the cost of traffic counting in urban areas, with the
help of automated systems. Another objective was to investigate existing systems regarding performance, accuracy,
cost, and so on. The comparisons were made more on general
methods for counting and registration, rather than involving
specific brand names. The conclusions reached were based
on field measurements, literature surveys, theoretical calculations and enquiries.

The field studies were carried out in Malmoe, the third
largest city in Sweden, in 1976 and included controlled
experiments as well as actual use in traffic. It is recommended that automated traffic counting is used at permanent
sites, with inductive loops as sensors. In order to mini-
mize the cost, only loops and boxes with connection and power supply should be installed at each site. Amplifiers,
detector logics and registration equipment should be circ-
ulated between different sites.

The following recommendations concerned the detector equipment. Inductive loops should be used with a loop length of
around 1.2-1.5 m. Detector logic should be used where
there is more than one loop, and one of the better systems
is the N+1 system. The detector amplifier ought to be self-
adjusting because, as has been shown in an Australian
study[3.1], more than 25% of the failures were due to getting
out of a site and readjusting the detectors.

The detector equipment should be built in modules, so that
one does not close up some modules in a site where counting
is not needed. For example, if one has a three-lane counting
station one does not want logics and detectors closed up in
that site.

Regarding data registers, the following conclusions were
reached. The reading of data should be possible at computer
terminals with the normally available equipment. One should
not have a special translator and extra equipment for translating data produced on the sites and to put into the computer. The best registers are those which have electronic
memories and one reader. When using magnetic tape cassettes
on each reader one ought to have the standard type, such as
EKMA 34. Stored information should be available at the
counting sites so that one knows what one is getting from the
sites. The equipment should be portable and in module form,
even for permanent sites.

The Swedish road administration is not so interested in classification in as many classes as say TRRL who uses approximately twenty-six classes. For most purposes it is sufficient to use three or four classes: ordinary vehicles, lorries, buses and bicycles. In order to simplify classification we tried using infra-red cells. We have found this to be quite successful for classification into two or three classes: ordinary vehicles, and lorries and buses. The error rate in classifying into two classes is approximately 1 - 2 % units.

We have tried the 3Ms, and have tried to nail the loops on the road, and to glue them with a textile tape which is very flexible. We have tried profile rubber mats with the loops inside. We have found that, for our purposes, moving around the measuring systems, and in daily measurement at intersections, lasting for up to a fortnight, if the traffic is about 30,000 per twenty-four hours, the best way is to put the loop on the surface and to use the textile tape. This has been quite successful.

Dr E. Smith (Department of Transport):

One hears a great deal about difficulties of automatic vehicle classification. The simplest form of classification is to put a classifier on the vehicle.

Often users do not want hourly flows but quarter-hourly flows though not for twenty-four hours, seven days a week and fifty-two weeks a year. Is there any possibility of having a machine which records the time after which a certain number of vehicles have passed, and then has a procedure for integrating this and converting to quarter-hourly periods at high flows and hourly periods at low flows?

Mr C. Maxwell-Stewart (TPA)

The cost of a permanent loop is very high and they are easily damaged. After installation one is inclined to stay with that heavy capital cost, even though circumstances may make it redundant. A temporary loop is therefore a very desirable development. Some years ago I was associated with a successful trial using a metallized tape as a temporary loop. The greatest problem was in getting the inductance correct; making it stand up enough to pick up the various types of vehicles. The actual technology in laying it out required a considerable amount of expertise by the technicians. Getting enough power to make them work was a problem. One would have to develop this quite a long way, matching sensitivity against power source.

Attempts to use something more permanent, like a metal tube, ran into the problem of Common Law. The highway authority might be liable for misfeasance if the tube broke and contributed to an accident. There have been actions in the High Court where highway authorities have been successfully sued in such matters.

We carried out some experiments on private roads on airfields, where we would be exempt from the provisions of Common Law in this respect. We found the deformation of the materials usually defeated us. Something sufficiently flexible to yield with the visco-elastic deformation of the pavement had to be used, but it could not be so flexible that it was abraded by the traffic, particularly when braked on.

Some of the tapes we put down can still be seen after about five years. They lasted only about one week in actual performance.

The other problem is that one has to take the output from the loop back to the recording device and, usually, coaxial cable has to be used to do this, otherwise the impulse is lost. That usually has to be put into some kind of chase. Having to do that, and particularly to get it across the drainage channel and up the kerb without having it protrude or causing an unseen hazard, presents some problems. The development was, however, abandoned because we felt it required more finance than we could reasonably produce. Nonetheless, at the stage we reached we were confident that there was sufficient basis for a solution.

Mr Gater (Paper 6)

With regard to temporary loops, bituthene material can equally well be used for holding down loop wires, and this would create less of a lump in the road than a pneumatic tube.

The breakage of the tube is not the worst thing that can happen; if there is a puncture in the tube, this can give distorted data and one cannot tell when the data became distorted.

Another temporary method is the use of Scotch Lane tape, which unfortunately is no longer available as a standard product. However if there was a greater demand more would be produced.

Another temporary technique which has been used is a rubber mat consisting of two pieces of synthetic rubber bounded together with the loop buried inside. This has to be held down firmly on the road, and this creates problems.

Mr A.W. Silver (Grampian Regional Council)

There is a colossal number of loops around the country, at

virtually all traffic control junctions and the approaches
to pelican crossings. We, as Engineers, are making no attempt
to make use of the loops which are already in place for us.
There is considerable scope here to do intermittent counting.

Little thought seems to have been given to the Local Authority data user who is already committed to a main frame computer system. There are no finances at the moment for desk
top systems which seem to be the priority especially in TRRL
development. There is a need for much closer co-operation
in looking at main frame systems rather than this continuing
fragmentation. Working towards a main frame, the days of
linking all the many computer data banks are not far away.
Rather than each organization maintaining separate data
information systems, we can all draw from one another.

Dr M.P. Heyes (Devon County Council)

One of the techniques that I have successfully used to install temporary loops is to cover them with a bitumastic material, similar to roofing felt. It has worked very successfully over long periods. A difficulty which did have to be
solved prior to using such installations for speed and headway measurements, was to be able to adjust the sensitivity
of the loops such that the effective distance between them
was the same as the actual distance on the road.

With respect to the debate about the best system for national traffic data collection, it is important to recognize
that the Counties have a considerable need for traffic data,
and the larger authorities, such as Devon, operate programmes
comparable with the National programmes. Although the technical ability to collect data automatically is becoming almost unlimited, as demonstrated (by the TRRL) I believe that
the critical problem is knowing what to do with the data.
So often in the past the collection of data has been used as
a device to avoid facing up to traffic and transport problems. This is particularly true of the urban transportation
studies where often two years and eleven months of a three
year study has been spent collecting data and analysing it,
and the last few weeks testing transportation strategies.
This trap should be carefully avoided.

Mr Y.H. Granne (Tyne and Wear County Council)

We in Tyne and Wear have for some time adopted the so-called
Chinese Finger as mentioned in Paper 7. When it was adopted
originally we carried out a trial and reduced the time that
the technicians needed to be on the road from well over half
an hour or three quarters of an hour to ten minutes. At

present we use a minimum of signing. We have a van with two
quartz halogen beacons placed on the top; we use portable
beacons on the highway in a tapering formation. The staff
use fluorescent jackets. This set-up is considered to be
perfectly safe.

Mr C.A. Cranley (Essex County Council)

There is a need for a reliable, indestructable, easily installed axle detector without mains. The configuration used
for signal approaches where signal loops are and where there
is stationary queueing traffic, gives a zero output for most
of the time.

Essex County Council have been attracted to the idea of
laying loops under resurfacing instead of slot-cutting. On
a ten-year programme for resurfacing it would be possible to
install, for almost next to nothing, loops throughout the
country.

Mr P. Rix (Devon County Council)

Regarding the installation of tubes in the road, is it fair
to say that with the introduction of the Health and Safety
at Work Act we are now, in the counties and the Department,
exposing technicians to what is a considerable hazard. There
is very little guidance in the way of signing or traffic control, which should be done in these circumstances.

Most local authorities probably have some sort of rule,
whereby the technicians go into the road when it is clear,
without introducing any signing at all. There is probably
nothing to say when they have to introduce signing and certainly not whether it should be exclamation marks or 'Men at
Work'. Some help would be welcome from the Department on
this matter.

Mr L.P. Jones   (Department of Transport, Manchester)

The North West Regional Office is in the process of installing a number of counting sites in the Region, particularly
on motorways. After a relatively short period of time it has
been found that the insulation resistance of loop conductors
to earth decreases quite appreciably, in some cases to about
one-hundredth of the figure specified by the Department which
is 10 megohms. An expert opinion needs to be given as to
what level of insulation resistance is acceptable for the
continuing satisfactory performance of the vehicle counting
equipment bearing in mind that once the loops are laid, it is
quite expensive to get a contractor to return to site and
carry out remedial measures which can be disruptive and cause
delays to traffic.

Mr Gater (Paper 6)

Without seeing the particular sites and examining any particular local problems, it is difficult to give a complete answer to Mr Jones' point. I have noticed, however, a number of things which can cause that kind of problem of reduction of resistance to earth. If the loop is not laid at the proper depth, small stones being forced through the bitumen surface can be forced through the insulation of the loop wires and cause leakage to earth. Problems will also be caused if the insulating material of the cable is not adequate for the job.

A suitable self-lubricating type of double insulation is quite important. If material like PVC is put in with hot bitumen, cracking of the insulation of the wire might be expected, either immediately or through time.

REFERENCES

3.1 Hulscher, F.R. (1974). Selection of vehicle detectors for traffic management. *Traff. Engng. Control, Dec.*

9. Trends in traffic data collection and analysis

J.A. Hillier, BSc(SPSO), D.H. Mathews, BSc, CChem, FRIC(PSO)
and R.C. Moore, (PSO)
Transport and Road Research Laboratory

The paper examines recent trends in the collection and use of
traffic data. Microprocessors enable a comprehensive range of
traffic data to be obtained. The results of surveys to establish central government data requirements are included. Time,
cost and error may be reduced by providing data in computer
compatible form for further analysis. A description of the
present methods of analysing the '50-Point' census data is
given, together with details of data vetting. Reservations are
expressed concerning the automatic data collection techniques
now becoming possible, particularly with regard to the
quantity and quality of data. The availability of microprocessor 'intelligence' at the roadside could allow traffic
management/control to be responsive to immediate conditions
and circumstances.

INTRODUCTION

1.   In identifying trends in traffic data collection and
analysis there are three main aspects to consider. First
there are changes in requirements for data, which arise
partly from policy development and associated research, and
partly from recognition of the potential of technical
developments in the instrumentation and data handling fields.
Second, there are the technical developments themselves,
which offer new possibilities in detection, measurement and
data manipulation. And thirdly, there are associated
changes in the techniques and procedures of analysis which
stem largely from the quantity and quality of the data that
the new technology provides.

2.   This paper examines these three aspects in turn.

DATA REQUIREMENTS

3.   A survey of the combined traffic data requirements of
TRRL and DTp Headquarters was conducted by TRRL in 1974 and

Table 1. Summary of surveys of data needs within DTp
Headquarters and TRRL

Type of measurement/data needed	Number of interested Divisions/Departments	
	HQ Divns	TRRL Depts
Traffic flow	11	6
Classification of traffic by type of vehicle	6	6
Speed	4	4
Following distance between vehicles	4	4
Axle-loads	8	2
Vehicle-loads	2	4
Axle-spacings	2	1
Vehicle-lengths	1	1
Transverse position (on carriageway)	2	3
Abnormal loads	2	1
Queue length	1	2
Accident data	4	2
Journey times	2	4
Journey-purpose data	2	4
Usage of vehicles	1	2
Details of road network	4	2
Amount of travel (vehicle-km)	1	2
Environmental conditions	2	1
Number of Divisions/Departments covered by surveys	17	6

was followed by more comprehensive surveys by DTp Headquarters in 1976 for the Working Group on Traffic Data
Collection. The combined results of these two surveys are
summarised in Table 1, with the exception of a few highly
specialised requirements (such as pedestrian flows, seat-
belt usage).

4. A point of general interest demonstrated by the table
is the amount and diversity of data required for research
purposes (i e TRRL). There are indeed no categories of
data required elsewhere in DTp which are not also needed
for research purposes; moreover, research generally demands
a specially high standard of accuracy and continuity of
data.

5. When compared with previous understanding of traffic data requirements, these surveys indicate a number of significant features. In the first place, there is increased emphasis on the classification of traffic counts by vehicle type. This, in part, arises because measures of driver behaviour such as speed and inter-vehicle gaps, for which there is an increasing need, and of vehicle characteristics, can be very much more informative when classified by vehicle type. It also arises because of requirements of the EEC, to enable the costs of road construction and maintenance to be attributed to the various classes of road user.

6. Second the tendency towards the use of larger and heavier goods vehicles, combined with the effects of restrictions in road building, has focused attention on road maintenance and on design standards. There is thus considerable emphasis on the need for data on axle weights and traffic composition on all classes of road, and on data relevant to the problem of traffic operation at road works.

7. Third, road safety research and the monitoring of road safety campaigns are calling for more and different types of information about road user behaviour and the associated road conditions. Thus routine data on traffic volumes, speeds and headways, together with the associated road configuration and environmental conditions are now required for a wide range of locations and times.

8. As the data requirements become more diverse in nature, there is also demand for larger and more representative samples. This may in part derive from the recognition that automatic counting, which is increasingly attractive, offers the opportunity to collect more data without heavy costs. But it also reflects the need to improve the prediction of future traffic demand, and to allow a higher degree of disaggregation in the various stages of analysis.

DEVELOPMENTS IN MEASUREMENT AND RECORDING

9. Present techniques used in data collection - such as traffic counters with pneumatic tube axle-detectors or loop detectors, radar meters for speed measurement, and dynamic weighbridges for measurements of axle-loads - tend to operate independently rather than in conjunction. In some cases, the on-site processing of the signals obtained from the sensors may be considerable, but each measurement is handled as a separate entity on a separate piece of equipment.

10. Considerable effort has been made by TRRL and Industry
to maximise the traffic information obtained from a single
loop sensor. The 'SCOOT' area traffic control scheme
employs a central computer to rapidly scan each loop and
from their status obtain details on average flows and queue
formation throughout an urban area. It seems likely that
some traffic data may in the future be obtained almost
incidently from urban areas employing area traffic control
methods. Overall costs in obtaining more comprehensive
data could be reduced, if the existing facilities (sensors,
detectors, power, GPO lines) were shared.

11. The present, wider need for traffic data provides a
new opportunity for the equipment designer to consider
what data is required (Table 1), and how to obtain maximum
data from each vehicle at minimum cost. Ultimately what
can be measured depends on the sensors, but by combining
the output from several it is possible to obtain quite
complex and detailed information about the total traffic
and about individual vehicles. It is believed that the key
to the practical realisation of such an installation is the
inclusion of a microprocessor as an integral part of on-
site instrumentation. A microprocessor can accept simultaneous inputs from a number of sensors, carry out computa-
tion on the inputs and thus produce an output of data which
may, if required, be in computer-compatible form for
further processing. The form, content and timing of the
output from the processor may be placed under the control
of the equipment user, so that only the data desired by
that user are collected. The data storage may be provided
on magnetic tape, memory or on a terminal printer. In the
future use may be made of solid state memory (bubble memory)
systems. The printer is especially useful for on-site
calibration, it may also conveniently be employed for
short duration collection of data and validation of magnetic
tape recording. It is also possible for the processor to
output data via a modem to GPO line for transmission to a
central computer. This ability to provide data in computer
compatible form, either on magnetic tape or by direct transmission, should enable substantial cost and time savings
to be made, and reduce errors produced by punching and
recoding data.

11. An inherent advantage of using a microprocessor-
controlled system for data collection is the flexibility it
can provide. A single piece of equipment may be used for
a variety of dissimilar tasks merely by changing the control
program. Thus, although the various surveys have indicated

what users think they may require, there is the possibility that these requirements will change and it is here that the adoption of microprocessor-based techniques should be of great advantage. If there are changes in the categories of vehicles to be classified, or if some users only seek a simplified classification then this can be handled without major changes in equipment. If new sensors are developed, the system would be in a position to take advantage of them.

12. To meet the requirement for increased samples of classified counts, associated with speeds, headways and axle weights, TRRL has developed a microprocessor-based vehicle classifier and count unit. A minicomputer was used to develop the software methodology, and a contract placed with industry to produce the microprocessor hardware. A typical detector array is an inductive loop, followed by an axle-detector and a second inductive loop with suitable electronic decoders connected to each. These allow the following data to be obtained for each vehicle: speed, length, wheelbase(s), overhang (length minus wheelbase) and a crude measure of chassis height. If axle-weight and total vehicle weight are required, then an additional road sensor (dynamic weighbridge) and electronic decoder unit are needed. The symmetry of the sensor arrangement will allow the equipment to accept two-directional flow, a facility that is important on two-way roads where overtaking is possible and also on unidirectional lanes if for any reason the direction of flow is reversed. However, the work so far has been confined to unidirectional flows and the software to handle two-way roads has yet to be developed. This microprocessor system and sensors can perform satisfactorily with vehicle speeds from 1 to 250 km/h, but if a vehicle stops over the sensors then incorrect classification is likely. This problem is being studied further.

13. The microprocessor vehicle classifier and count equipment output may be vehicle-by-vehicle or in summary form. The detailed output is essential during calibration and validation of the classification techniques and may also be useful in meeting the requirements of some users (eg, time intervals, sequence of heavily laden vehicles). A summarised output can be obtained at predetermined intervals of time and its content can be specified by means of the software. Choices will at least include: vehicle count/ class/lane, total flow/lane, commercial flow/lane, average speed/class/lane, average weight/class/lane, and the number of axles/class exceeding a preset weight level. The types of vehicle which may be separately classified are shown in Figure 1.

131

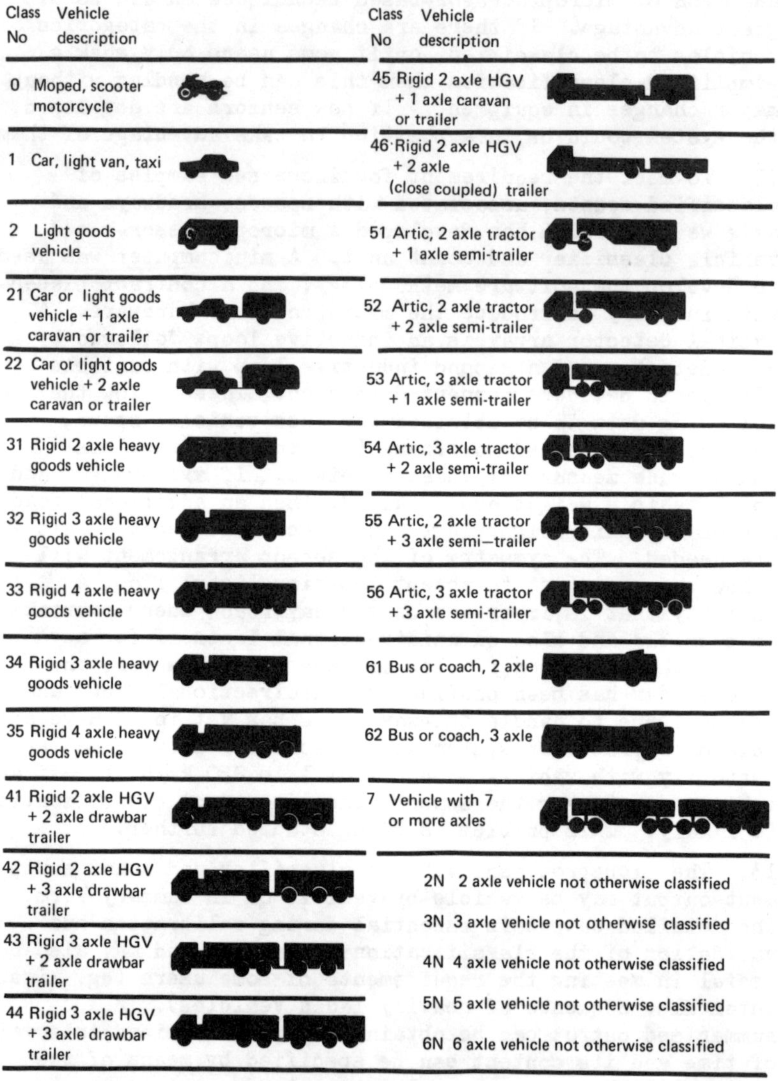

Class No	Vehicle description		Class No	Vehicle description	
0	Moped, scooter motorcycle		45	Rigid 2 axle HGV + 1 axle caravan or trailer	
1	Car, light van, taxi		46	Rigid 2 axle HGV + 2 axle (close coupled) trailer	
2	Light goods vehicle		51	Artic, 2 axle tractor + 1 axle semi-trailer	
21	Car or light goods vehicle + 1 axle caravan or trailer		52	Artic, 2 axle tractor + 2 axle semi-trailer	
22	Car or light goods vehicle + 2 axle caravan or trailer		53	Artic, 3 axle tractor + 1 axle semi-trailer	
31	Rigid 2 axle heavy goods vehicle		54	Artic, 3 axle tractor + 2 axle semi-trailer	
32	Rigid 3 axle heavy goods vehicle		55	Artic, 2 axle tractor + 3 axle semi—trailer	
33	Rigid 4 axle heavy goods vehicle		56	Artic, 3 axle tractor + 3 axle semi-trailer	
34	Rigid 3 axle heavy goods vehicle		61	Bus or coach, 2 axle	
35	Rigid 4 axle heavy goods vehicle		62	Bus or coach, 3 axle	
41	Rigid 2 axle HGV + 2 axle drawbar trailer		7	Vehicle with 7 or more axles	
42	Rigid 2 axle HGV + 3 axle drawbar trailer		2N	2 axle vehicle not otherwise classified	
43	Rigid 3 axle HGV + 2 axle drawbar trailer		3N	3 axle vehicle not otherwise classified	
44	Rigid 3 axle HGV + 3 axle drawbar trailer		4N	4 axle vehicle not otherwise classified	
			5N	5 axle vehicle not otherwise classified	
			6N	6 axle vehicle not otherwise classified	

Fig. 1   TRRL VEHICLE CLASS LISTING COMPATIBLE WITH EEC
REGULATION R1108/70

14. An indication of the accuracy of vehicle classification using a prototype microprocessor is given in Table 2 for a small sample of vehicles on the M4 motorway. Some categories of vehicle were not present in this sample, it is however the most recent calibration available. Measurements on speed accuracy showed an average speed error of $\pm$ 0.5 mph with a standard deviation of 2 mph. Average length error was 0.31m for cars, and 0.28m for commercial vehicles. Average wheelbase error was 0.1m for all vehicles.

15. The estimated cost of a microprocessor-based system, including the costs for purchase and installation of the necessary sensors in the road together with the decoding units and housings for all the equipment, is £2,900 for a 2-lane carriageway and £4,200 for a 4-lane site. In each case it is assumed that the output will be recorded on magnetic tape cassette and the price (£500) of the necessary unit is included in the estimate.

APPLICATION OF THE NEW TECHNIQUES

16. Discrimination between most of the common types (and some less common) of vehicle is now possible with automatic equipment although there remain some categories where there is a risk of misclassification. Such errors tend to be consistent rather than spread over a number of classes in a random manner. In a few cases, such as 2-wheelers which are of interest in accident studies, it is not possible to sub-divide the classification in as much detail as is obtained manually because the physical differences between the different types of vehicle are fairly fine. It seems likely that some limited manual check will be needed to deal with these problems of misclassification or insufficient classification.

17. The use of the classifier has so far been confined to dual-carriageways where the problems posed by variations in vehicle path are not usually severe. Techniques remain to be defined for 2-way roads where, for example, overtaking and deflection of vehicle paths by parked vehicles can pose serious problems even with present counters. Site selection seems likely to become even more critical than it is at present. When there are several parameters to be measured, there could well be a conflict between the requirements for site position. Certainly the existing locations for regular traffic counting will need careful reconsideration when contemplating the installation of classification equipment.

Table 2. Classification of microprocessor unit.
M4 motorway 27-10-77 and 9-11-77

Class No.	Sample Size	Correct %	Incorrect %
0	4	100	–
1	754	94.5	5.5
21	17	59	41
22	2	50	50
31	400	94.5	5.5
32	41	95	5
33	38	97.5	2.5
41	2	100	–
45	2	50	50
51	52	92	8
52	229	94	6
54	4	–	100
55	7	–	100
61	13	83	17

18. Increasing problems will be caused at the permanent
data collection sites because sensors and the necessary
connecting cables will be buried in the road surface. This
has already given rise to quite important reliability and
maintenance problems, especially in urban areas. For
example, in an ATC system in Glasgow there were 135 sensor
installations and on average only 90 per cent were
operational at any time with a mean time between failures
of only 7 days. A survey of sensor reliability at 20 sites
operated by TRRL on motorways over the 4 years 1972-76
showed that there were 72 break-downs of which 25 per cent
were caused by power or sensor loop cables being cut or
damaged. All cables and sensors buried in the surface of
the road are at risk, and anything that can be done to
develop less vulnerable detection techniques will be of
great benefit.

ANALYSIS OF DATA FROM AUTOMATIC COUNTERS

19. Automatic counters, capable of giving classified
counts together with related data on driver behaviour and
vehicle characteristics, seem certain to replace most manual
counting at least at permanent counting sites. Their
availability, coupled with the requirements for more
comprehensive data, will also encourage the setting-up of
many more counting stations. The resulting increase in the
quantity of data to be handled, coupled with the operational

characteristics of the equipment involved, require special procedures for interpretation and analysis, and an efficient organisation for installation and maintenance.

20. The Laboratory has for some years now, been involved in the day-to-day running of a permanent data collection system - the 50-point census. The census is based on the use of simple automatic counters which provide unclassified counts without additional data. However the operation of such a census - from the supervision and maintenance of automatic counters on site, to the complex task of processing the incoming data - is far from straightforward. Although superficially a census system may seem to be a simple sequential chain of events - counter operation, data recording and transmission and data handling, storage and analysis (as required) - in practice the various elements in the chain are interactive. The way in which data is collected has important implications for its subsequent processing and analysis: checks made during processing provide essential feedback information for monitoring the earlier data collection and transmission stages. The census operation should therefore be regarded as a total system, and designed in the light of the interactive nature of the various stages. It is a weakness of some current systems that this is not done.

21. In order to illustrate the points made in the previous paragraph, the 50-point census system will be briefly described, emphasizing the total system aspect, and the implications for a larger more comprehensive data acquisition system will be outlined.

22. Figure 2 illustrates the 50-point census system. The system was designed to monitor travel trends on the national road network (excluding motorways and unclassified roads), and is based on a sample of 50 counting stations distributed over trunk and classified roads in Great Britain. Each counting station is equipped with a recording counter (Fischer and Porter) which records hourly flows on punched paper tapes. The counters are supervised by agents (usually Local Authorities), who undertake regular (weekly or fortnightly) counter checks and who send the completed tapes each month to the Laboratory. The counter agents also provide routine reports of counter operation and other information of relevance to the flow data (eg local events, weather, roadworks and road improvements) which is essential to the interpretation of the data in the analysis stages. Counter agents will also undertake minor

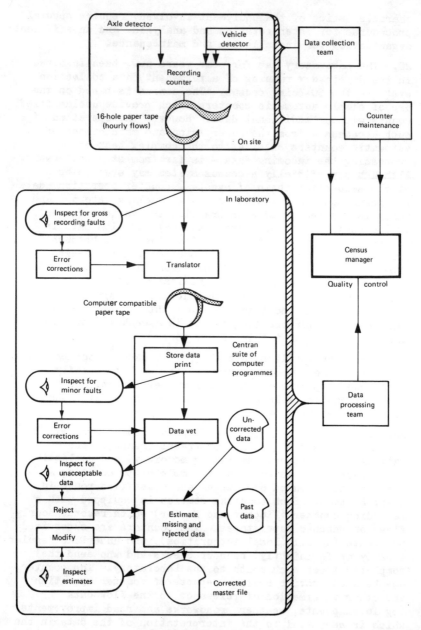

Fig. 2 THE 50 POINT CENSUS SYSTEM

repairs or adjustments to counters, but major repairs and replacements are carried out by a specialist maintenance group centred at the Laboratory.

23. Once the primary data tapes (16-hole paper) have been received at the Laboratory an elaborate system of checking, translation and processing begins. The tapes are first physically checked for obvious errors, such as faulty punching or other equipment dependant faults. The 16-hole tape is then translated (together with the gross error corrections) to produce computer compatible paper tapes. A print-out of these input tapes is examined for further errors arising from both human and mechanical sources. It has been found that although some of these errors could be detected automatically later in the processing, it is more efficient and less expensive to vet the data carefully in the early stages. Both of these initial error detection stages not only allow errors to be corrected early in the processing cycle, but provides essential feed back to the counter agents or the maintenance group to identify counter malfunctions. An important example of data errors is a timing shift, when data collected during a particular hour is attributed (punched) to another hour. This type of error may be due to a faulty counter mechanism, but is more usually an operator fault. Having detected such a timing shift it is a relatively simple matter to move the data in the computer file. A more difficult problem - both for detection and correction - arises when the flow data is suspected of being higher or lower than expected. Here the reports from counter agents giving local information is of prime importance and this information when coupled with familiarity with the site and its neighbourhood can usually indicate possible cause and suggest error correcting procedures.

24. However carefully the data is vetted and errors corrected, there will inevitably be gaps in the data (due to breakdowns) and data which has to be rejected because it cannot be satisfactorily corrected. Because the aim of the 50-point census processing is to provide full hourly flow data for every site, any missing data has to be estimated. This task is probably the most difficult of all. The most important requirement is that there should be a complete record of site characteristics, past flow data and past equipment performance, supplemented by a knowledge of the place of the road in the local road network and any local events which might affect flows. In simple cases - where only a few hours counts are missing or perhaps one or more

days counts - it may be possible to estimate missing data by linear interpolation. This technique must however be used with care since there are a number of periods of the year when changes in traffic flow with time are far from linear.

25. The CENTRAN suite of computer programs used to process the 50-point census provides an alternative method which is based on a growth rate correction factor applied to past data for the corresponding day of the year. A more recently developed estimating technique can be applied to sites where separate directional counts are available (eg dual carriageways). This method is based on the finding that the ratio of the directional daily flows for a particular day of the week remains stable in time. Experience in using this method has shown that on dual carriageway sites the method is satisfactory for estimating missing daily flows, and hourly flows can be interpolated using past hour flow data and growth rate factors calculated from the daily flows.

FUTURE

26. An essential element in present methods of automatic classification is the axle-detector. In the development trials pneumatic tube detectors have been used but they are not suitable where there are three or more lanes on the carriageway, or for permanent installations. They may be suitable in temporary installations where the short life of the detector is of minor consequence. The Laboratory has discussed with industry the need to develop a satisfactory axle-detector; in addition several prototypes have been designed. Some of these prototypes are operational at a test site on M4 (installed in September 1977) and two (installed February 1977) at a site on A40.

27. At temporary sites it will be necessary to use portable sensors, detectors and signal processing equipment to enable the collection of data covering most of the range possible at more permanent locations, including axle-weights. There is a particular need for a portable weighing pad. A device to provide even a very crude separation by axle-load (eg a count of axles exceeding 5 tons) would be of great help to some users. It is hoped to produce such a transducer in the near future. One of the problems of the use of portable equipment is power supply, even with low consumption electronic units. It seems unlikely that it will normally be economic to provide mains. For each application there will be a generally accepted period over which data must be

collected, which will have a direct bearing on power supplies. At present, it is being assumed that data will be collected for at least a week before moving the equipment elsewhere.

28. A note of warning should be sounded about the data collection capabilities now becoming possible. It will be necessary to consider carefully what sorts of data are really needed and in how much detail for any particular application. The cost of gathering the data will be broadly similar whether a vehicle-by-vehicle output or just a summary is required, but the effort and costs involved in storing and processing the data subsequently could be very different. There is a danger that quantity could become a substitute for quality so that the value of having a wider statistical basis would be undermined. Indeed, in some applications such as the national traffic censuses, one of the major problems to be resolved is how to handle the vastly increased quantity of data whilst maintaining a high standard in the processing and checking. Experience with the 50-point census has shown that it is well worth while taking considerable care to detect and correct the faults that are inevitable at some time with automatic data collection. The possibility which now exists of direct transfer of the data by telephone line on to a central processor for storage and analysis, is possibly more relevant to fault detection and convenience than it is to the need to make data available much more quickly. If data is required immediately on a particular site, then the on-site printer may well be the most suitable solution. However, the rapid detection of faults has obvious implications in terms of the efficiency and scale of the data collection. Much thought still needs to be given to what is the best balance of transfer of the data to the main processor. Localised magnetic storage, site by site, has the advantage that site visits are needed to collect the tapes and there is some local contact. Some visits are almost certainly going to be necessary to carry out equipment checks not possible from the remote centre and until the frequency of such visits can be established, it is difficult to be too categorical on how the data may be best transmitted between site and processor.

29. The data collection applications discussed in the previous sections are largely passive as far as the traffic itself is concerned. However, the most important merit of a microprocessor is its ability to control processes in real time, and it is this property which may

lead to the greatest changes in the use of traffic data.
Traffic control can be made responsive to immediate
conditions and circumstances because 'intelligence' is
available on site. Many microprocessor applications will
increase the convenience or economy of existing procedures
such as traffic surveys and passive censuses, but the big
step will be their use to assess or predict undesirable
traffic conditions and to call up the appropriate control
measures. For example, a particular distribution of
following distances, vehicle mix and speed might turn out
to be closely related to the risk of shock-wave shunts.
Undesirable concentrations of axle loads might be dispersed
before passing over bridges under repair.

30. Finally it is worth emphasizing that a data gathering
system must be designed as a whole in respect of technical
and management aspects if a high quality of data is to be
obtained. The more complex the system, the greater the
need for careful design and for proper control in operation.
The successful application of automatic traffic data equipment on a large scale requires a special management .
structure, with a good feel for the operational problems
and an appropriate blend of skills in engineering, data
processing and statistics.

10. Future proposals for the automatic collection and retrieval of traffic data - its potential and problems

R. Ham
Department of Transport

SYNOPSIS. Many possibilities are being offered by new technology for the collection of vital traffic data. The capabilities of this new technology are almost limitless provided that the costs are acceptable and that a clear definition of fundamental requirements can be made at the outset. To illustrate these points and to give a flavour of what might be achieved, this paper describes a system for the centralised collection of traffic data and discusses both the advantages and the problems which would be encountered.

INTRODUCTION

1. The collection, analysis and utilisation of traffic census is carried out by Central Government, Local Government and other bodies for a variety of purposes. Since, in many instances, they work independently of each other some duplication of effort inevitably occurs and this is wasteful of resources. The cost of present labour-intensive data collection methods is becoming unacceptable and doubts have been raised as to their accuracy. A national automatic data collection and retrieval system for traffic census purposes would enable all potential users to have access to a nationally distributed chain of vehicle counting and vehicle classification census sites. This paper proposes one such system and considers both it's potential and possible problems.

2. The proposed system would be based on the use of inductive loop vehicle detector equipment, line communications, and local and central computer systems. It exploits the results of the recent significant developments in these fields. It draws upon the

experience of the Traffic Control and Communications
Division of the Department of Transport in computer systems
and line communications techniques and in the technology
of inductive loop vehicle detection systems gained since
the initial evaluation study in 1964, both for traffic
counting and in the more demanding field of traffic control
and automation.

3. While in the main the paper is concerned with the
automatic collection of data, it is recognised that manual
collection of data may be appropriate for some time to
come, and that provision must be made for this. The
proposed retrieval network would be based on small
computers which would both automatically collect the raw
traffic data and carry out some initial processing to
present this to the user in forms which were immediately
meaningful and useful for his particular application.

4. The growth of the road network has led to an
increasing demand for traffic data of high quality, both
nationally and locally. The proposed system concentrates
on obtaining data for national purposes from a sample of
roads to suit those needs. However, there is no reason
why it could not be expanded to cater for more local needs
by the addition of additional collection sites.

THE SYSTEM

5. The system objective would be to make data readily
available to all users, with the following advantages:-

   a. a reduction in the manpower required to collect
      the data;

   b. an increase in data availability and accuracy;

and c. greater convenience and flexibility for users
      in obtaining access to the data which they
      require.

6. The system would provide far more data on a continuous
basis than is available at present. It would use a
network of field stations to collect the required data
and to pass it to a central data collection system.

7. The central data system would check validity and would
sort and structure the data before carrying out initial
analysis to make it suitable for users. The users of data
would gain access to the system in several ways depending
on their needs including the frequency at which data was
required. For frequent users, data terminals could be

provided giving them direct access to the system from their own premises. Such access could take one of several forms, including arrangements which would provide data which could be fed directly into another computer system for further analysis.

8. The basic unit of the system would be the automatic traffic data collection field station installed at each of the selected sites. The number of traffic parameters to be automatically monitored would determine the complexity of the monitoring equipment installed at a particular field station. The requirements might range from simple vehicle counting (volumetric) to fairly complex vehicle classification. In the future additional data might be required, for example information on environmental and road conditions such as the presence of fog, rain, ice or snow.

9. At the time of writing this paper vehicle classification systems have only undergone comparatively brief trials. However, a number of more permanent test sites have been installed from which results on the accuracy and reliability of automatic classification systems should shortly become available. When adequate experience of such equipment has been gained it will allow the development of a micro-computer based field station capable of either vehicle classification or simple volumetric counting. This 'standard' field station can then be universally installed at all census sites to allow some of the economies associated with large scale production to be realised. Such economies can be anticipated since the actual costs of micro-computers is small compared to the cost of programming (which is a 'once only' task). In addition, where only simple volumetric counting is required, more economic road sensor arrays than those which are required for vehicle classification may be installed.

10. The typical field station for use within the system would probably consist of 2 micro-computers connected together. The first micro-computer would have the task of determining the data required, eg counting or classifying vehicles. The second micro-computer would restructure the data into a form suitable for data communication, and would compress it to reduce the amount of data which actually had to be transmitted. This second micro-computer would also perform all the data communication functions.

11. When a field station could not, for various reasons, be connected directly to the central system, an on-site data recorder would be added to the basic field station configuration and the line communication equipment would be removed. The basic capability of a standard field station unit to provide for remote data collection or on-site collection is extremely important. Apart from the economies of allowing one type of field station to be used for all purposes, it would also permit the provision of a national network to take place gradually, starting with the field station as the most important element. This is a very substantial advantage.

12. It is important to further stress the desirability of a universal field station. This would allow the same electronic equipment to be supplied irrespective of the data being collected. This would give three advantages:

>   1. The larger quantity of one design being produced would reduce the unit cost of the equipment.
>
>   2. It would be possible to alter the data collected on site from the central system without having to visit the sites (assuming that the full sensor package has been provided).
>
>   3. Maintenance problems would be simplified with a single design; the quantity of spares holdings would also be reduced.

This common field station would also be used for sites where the data is recorded locally.

13. Figure 1 shows the basic system configuration. The heart of the system would be a central mini-computer which would perform the main data storage and analysis functions and which would generally control the whole system. Around this mini-computer would be a number of micro-computers which would communicate directly with the field stations. Users terminals would also be connected to the mini-computer system

SYSTEM OPERATION

14. The field station's main function is to collect the necessary traffic data. At many sites this will mean that details of a vehicle's class, its speed, and the gap between it and the vehicle in front are recorded. At the same time details of road and weather conditions may be recorded. The field station will also be continually

carrying out self-checking routines to ensure that all
equipment is functioning correctly. There are a number
of techniques for automatically checking the operation of
vehicle detection equipment, and these can be relatively
inexpensive if designed into the system from the start.
Such checks would ensure that all vehicle detectors were
responding correctly to vehicles. The correct operation
of the system to a testing schedule would be carried out
at periodic intervals. Traffic data would be stored
on-site in short term storage for a period of up to 24
hours, so that all data need only be retrieved from that
site once per day.

15. Recovery of data from sites would be controlled by
the regional sector micro-computer. Field stations would
be connected back to the central system by line communications, but the actual method would vary considerably
depending on the location of the station. Most field
stations would be connected to the central system via the
normal Post Office switched telephone network. Field
stations installed on motorways would be connected via
the motorways communication system to the national
motorway control centre which would retrieve the data from
all motorway sites and pass it to the central data system
over a single data link. Where field stations are installed
within the boundaries of an Urban Traffic Control (UTC)
System, connection of these sites may take place using the
UTC system communications network, again with a single
data collection link between the UTC system and the
central data system.

16. Once per day the regional sector computer would
obtain all the traffic data for the preceding 24 hours.
As the majority of this data collection would be via the
public telephone network this operation would take place
between midnight and 6.00 am to take advantage of the
period when telephone exchange equipment is least busy
and to benefit from the Post Office's "Midnight Line"
cheap tariff. Retrieving traffic data at this time also
means that information on the previous day's traffic flow
is available at the start of the working day. The
regional sector micro-computer would automatically call
(ie dial) the telephone number of each field station in
turn to retrieve both the traffic data and the results
of the system's self-checking routine. This micro-
computer would then restructure the data from all the
field stations in its sector before passing it to the
central computer.

17. On receipt of this data the mini-computer would check its validity. It would first examine the replies received from the on-site checking routines, and would then continue the process by looking in more detail at the actual data received. Trends in the data would be compared to recent trends from the same site and from adjacent sites. This fairly simple technique will indicate when there may be cause for doubting the validity of the data and on some occasions may give indications of error where none exists. When an error indication has been given it will be possible for an operator to inspect the data and to use his skill to judge whether the data should be used and the error message ignored, whether the data is in error for some transient reason and should be rejected, or whether an one-site check should be made.

18. Once the data validity has been established some preliminary analysis may be carried out. This would consist initially of the summation of daily totals for each site, which can then be added to weekly, monthly or annual totals. These totals could be used with the information from other field sites to give regional totals. They could then be used with other analysis programs to give projections for traffic flows in other areas, general trends and, possibly, future predictions. However, because of the complexity of such analyses, and the variety of different forms in which users may require their data, they would normally be carried out separately by the user's main computers once the data has been retrieved from the system.

19. The final role of the central system would be to provide the data in a form in which it can most readily be used. For example, if a user requires daily totals, it would be extremely wasteful to provide him with figures for each 15 minute period. The computer would therefore sort the data into a repertoire of pre-arranged formats which the user could request. For regular users a data terminal would be provided on his premises with which he could gain access to the central system. Depending on the frequency of use and the amount of data required, this connection would either be by rented private wire or, again, by dialled telephone line. Once a user had achieved connection he would request the output required and the format desired.

20. It is of interest to consider briefly some of the technical capabilities of the system. I have described a

central system which consists of a mini computer and a number of small micro-computers (figure 1). I have done this deliberately to show the flexibility of the system. The micro-computers could undoubtedly be dispensed with if a larger computer was used at the centre. However, the distributed power of the system described will give a higher degree of reliability. If one of the major aims of this system is to provide a data service which can obtain continuous traffic data without significant gaps, the system must guard against the failure of the equipment at the central location.

21. This can most easily be achieved with the configuration shown. Two examples of failure may be used to illustrate this point. Firstly, if the mini-computer itself fails, particularly in the middle of the night during the critical period when the data is being gathered - and there were no micro-computers - all data from throughout the country for a 24 hour period would be lost. With this proposal the micro-computers will still carry on collecting that data and although they will be unable to pass it on to the mini-computer no data will be lost since the micro-computers will store it. Provided that the main computer is back in service before it is time to collect the next days data, no data will be lost. Such an arrangement therefore gives a 24 hour period in which repairs can take place.

22. The second example assumes a failure of one of the regional sector micro computers. In these circumstances its functions would be automatically taken over by its neighbours. Each micro-computer will have the ability to collect data from a share of its neighbours sector but will not normally carry out this function. In the event of failure this capability will be used to ensure that no data is lost.

23. The other main advantage of the proposed configuration is that the mini-computer is free to carry out analysis routines and service data users requirements without having to carry out the arduous and time consuming routine associated with the use of data collection on dialled telephone lines. This arrangement will have the added advantage that should some users (possibly those associated with traffic control) require more immediate data, then the configuration shown will make it possible for the system to obtain from site the very latest data.

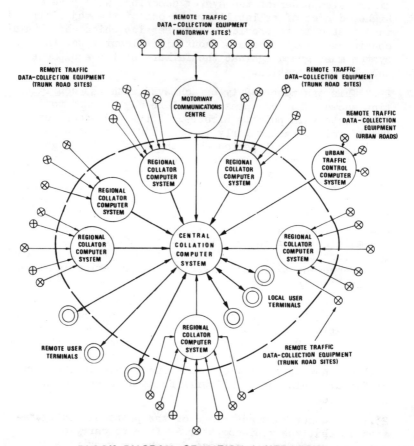

BLOCK DIAGRAM OF NATIONAL NETWORK
FOR TRAFFIC CENSUS DATA COLLECTION

Fig 1

SYSTEM POTENTIAL

24. I have described so far a system for automatically collecting traffic data and making it readily available to the user; the enormous potential of this system is largely self evident. However, it may be of interest to briefly highlight a few particular points.

25. Firstly, the scale of the proposed system. In describing it I have had in mind a system encompassing roughly the existing Departmental 200 point census. But if there is a justifiable need for continuous collection of data then there is no reason why the system could not encompass all 1800 or so points of the various present Departmental census. The system could also cater for the more localised needs of local authorities and to this end many more local sites could be introduced to the system. All these needs could be met within a single co-ordinated system, which would then provide standardised arrangements for data collection with a high quality, reliable service.

26. If such a system expansion is to be possible however, it is important that this is recognised from the start. Even if the system is introduced with only a few data collection sites some provision must be made for its future expansion. If adequate provision is not made from the outset any subsequent expansion may be difficult, expensive or indeed, impossible.

27. The system should also be able to cater for a wide range of users. In addition to the regular Departmental and local authority users, research bodies such as universities would also be able to utilise the data available. Although it may not be possible for such organisations to justify having a terminal, they could obtain data from nearby terminal users or by the postal services ("Datapost").

28. Since the system will contain data that has not been available before, particularly on a continuous basis, it will now meet the needs of such interests as road safety. Where vehicle classification sites are installed they will have the ability to measure vehicle speeds and inter-vehicle gaps. Such data will be available for all periods of the day and can be related to weather conditions and traffic levels.

29. The data can also be of value to traffic control authorities. Since the system will contain data which is less than 24 hours old it should be possible to use it in

the formulation of day to day control strategies. This will be particularly useful at sites on approaches to urban areas and possibly, in the future, on motorways.

30. As the central system is computer based it obviously has the potential to carry out much more detailed and complex analysis before presenting the data to the user. It also has the ability to operate in an inter-active mode enabling the user to make the system carry out routines to suit his particular needs at that time and to keep changing the type of analysis carried out, possibly by trial and error method, until the required results are obtained. In other words the system could be expanded to become part of a large, all ambracing traffic data bank able to meet the needs of almost all users. Technically this arrangement could be achieved with the present state of the art. However, I feel that a degree of caution may be necessary here and this is discussed further in the next section on system problems.

31. As a final 'potential' of this system, it is worth considering in the longer term an ultimate development which is an alternative to the previous possibility. Although there are advantages in keeping the system dedicated to the task of obtaining traffic data and processing it only in so far as to make it appropriate to the users needs, it could take on a further role to give an overall system of much greater capability. The system could be linked to other computer processing systems, so that it would pass its data, upon request from a user, to some remote processing system, and then recover the processed data from that computer and pass it to the user. With the powerful computer systems currently available, data could be moved from system to system to give an extremely flexible processing arrangement, which would have the capability of meeting all types of user needs.

SYSTEM PROBLEMS

32. So far this paper has sketched a fairly attractive picture of the capabilities of an automatic traffic data collection and retrieval system, and the facilities and services that it would provide for the user. However there are problems which must be considered.

33. One of the major attractions of such a system is the great reduction in the labour needed to collect traffic data with its attendant high costs. But the system would not entirely eliminate the use of manual counters.

However extensive the equipment and the validity checking which is carried out by the automatic system, it will not be able to determine all the faults, nor will it be able to detect with absolute certainty that incorrect data is not being received, (for example, because of roadworks blocking part of the road very near to the census site). Under such conditions the results provided by the counter equipment are likely to be inaccurate but could be masked in any automatic validation system. Manual counting teams will therefore still be required, firstly to collect data in the event of failure of the automatic equipment and secondly, to carry out periodic manual counts at each site to check the validity of the automatic counts.

34. It must also be recognised that it will not be possible, in the forseeable future, to collect all types of traffic data automatically. Provision will therefore have to be made for the manual collection of such data and for its input into the system. An example of this is origin and destination data which will need manual involvement.

35. Before attempting to design an automatic data collection system the fundamental limitations of present day traffic data collection equipment must be recognised. The siting limitations on vehicle counting equipment are comparatively well known, but the limitations on the use of vehicle classification equipment may be more severe. Vehicle classification equipment will probably only perform reliably in situations where traffic is free-flowing and where lane discipline is reasonably good. This will mean that some sites from which vehicle classified data is required will have to be carefully considered to decide whether the precise location of the site should be changed to one more suitable for automatic classification, or, if the location of the site cannot be changed, then manual vehicle classification may still have to be used.

36. A high calibre of staff will be needed to plan and specify this system, before a detailed design can be considered. It is essential that the system designers are of a suitable calibre if the system is to be installed without major problems or limitations. Although the staff needed to operate and maintain the system will be greatly reduced, those actually employed will probably have to be more skilled than those used at present. Nevertheless considerable savings should accrue.

37. Finally, to perhaps the most significant problem. From the main description and the section on system

operation, it will be seen that the system has great flexibility and a considerable capability for expansion. But caution is necessary. It will not be possible for users of data to opt now for a system which can collect data from say 10 or 20 sites on a simple vehicle count basis with perhaps a simple print out at the central location, and, at the same time, to expect in the future to expand this to a full system servicing several hundred or more sites. It is vital that the ultimate capacity and capability of the system is defined and that this is planned for from its inception. The ability of the system to be expanded in stages would, if necessary, allow it to be installed gradually without the need for a very large initial expenditure. But this ability will not relieve the project planner from the responsibility of obtaining from the users a complete picture of their needs in the ultimate system if a suitable system configuration is to be determined. This will entail all planned users of the system deciding on what their requirements will be and on reaching agreement on how the data should be analysed and presented. Without this, the system may not be expandable from its small beginnings, or if it can be extended it may be far less efficient, more expensive, and will almost inevitably impose unnecessary limitations on the user.

38. Mention has also been made of the possibility of being able to carry out much more complex data analysis routines within the one system. There would be a number of problems with this type of approach. Firstly, complex analysis routines can absorb considerable amounts of computer time. With a large number of users there are likely to be many different routines. Difficulties involving a conflict of priorities could arise when a number of users were trying to gain access to the system at one time. The basic system described, with its ability to collect vast quantities of data and make it available for the user to carry out his own analysis with his own computer, is the type of system which could be designed and installed with minimal administrative and engineering problems. However, the inclusion of complex analysis routines in the system would make both the design and implementation much more difficult, and satisfactory commissioning would become a protracted activity. Finally, since the individual user will undoubtedly wish to make changes to his analysis routines at fairly frequent intervals to take into account his changes of requirements, considerable administrative problems could be posed for

a very large central system because of the wide range of users. The system could end up in a state of almost continual modification.

CONCLUSION

39. This paper proposes a system for automatically collecting traffic data; bringing it back to a central location; and making it readily available to users. It has given some indication of the very wide capabilities of such a system whilst identifying some of the problems which must be recognised and considered at the planning stage if later difficulties are to be avoided. None of these problems is insurmountable and with careful planning from the outset it would undoubtedly be possible to achieve a very effective system. From a purely technical aspect, such a system need not be a long way off. It is anticipated that a small pilot data collection and retrieval system, intended to demonstrate basic capabilities, will have been installed and will be operating by the time of this Conference.

40. One of the functions of the DTp Traffic Control and Communications Division is to define standards for systems of the type proposed in this Paper -. by means of technical Specifications, etc. With this responsibility in mind, I would like to stress one final point.

41. With the capabilities of present technology, and of that which is emerging from current research and development, it is not unreasonable to claim that virtually any need which may be specified by the data user can be met. The limiting factors are cost and, to a lesser extent, time. Against this background neither the user nor the equipment supplier can be expected to specify, sensible performance requirements unilaterally. An effective, on-going dialogue between the two parties, as has been initiated at this Conference, is essential. Thus the user can give an initial statement of his general needs, to which the equipment designer can respond with tentative designs and cost estimates. This will allow the user to amend his demand as necessary for further consideration by the designer, and so on. From this refining process it should be possible to arrive at a final system which will provide the user with the most appropriate solution for his needs within his cost constraints, whilst ensuring that all relevant techniques are recognised and exploited.

42. Such an iterative dialogue is particularly vital to reach a satisfactory statement of requirements for overall system accuracy and reliability, where cost versus capability decisions may be very keen. At the end of the day specifications will have to be prepared to give clear, definitive operational and design requirements for the system.

Discussion on Papers 9 and 10

The Chairman

Why do you not test the automatic equipment against a known input on the TRRL track?

Mr Hillier (Paper 9)

To simulate a three lane motorway on the TRRL test track with the variety of vehicle classes required would be very expensive. Film analysis of the existing M4 motorway site is a more attractive method of confirming the accuracy of the automatic classifying equipment.

Mr F. Mulder (Traffic Management Systems, Netherlands)

Traffic Management Systems is not only a manufacturer but acts as a consultants office, used free of charge by the government. Very often one works perhaps two years to try to find equipment, only to learn that the government have changed their mind or go to another manufacturer.

Holland is a very small country compared with England, and the responsibility for the highways rests with one department for the whole country; the official governmental department. This department not only does the counting but also the research, putting out specifications, putting into operation and maintaining the equipment. It is more or less a combination of TRRL, the counties, and the rest together.

The provincial roads are the responsibility of the local authorities. Six years ago, the government started to renew the equipment for data collection on the main roads. They started with about sixty measuring points, with punched tape recorders. In addition, they bought ten magnetic tape recorders and, with the help of these recorders, they were able to measure the speed, length, the gap time between two cars and the distance between two cars. Besides this equip-

ment, they also had two completely equipped mobile cars, with
PDPL computers and video tape. After six years, they put all
the information together and found out that although it was
good to have all this information there was too much.

They decided that it was enough for the Dutch market to
have a classification of three length categories, and ten
speed categories. After taking this decision, the punched
tape recorder equipment was replaced by equipment which will
classify all the incoming information. At the same time,
the old mechanical counters were replaced on the highways by
completely electronic counters with an exchangeable solid
state memory.

J.A. Bailey (GEC-Elliott Traffic Automation Ltd)

Data has been collected in a number of industries over a
considerable time, and the problem has shown itself to be in
two parts:
  (a)   The necessity to put sufficient investment in an
        instrument to collect the information.
  (b)   The requirement to standardize on the information to
        be collected.
There are many instances in which a non-coordinating industry
has been incapable of finding sufficient finance in order to
develop measuring equipment whereas others contributing
together have solved the problem. A simple example of a non-
coordinated industry is shown in the paper industry where
water content needs to be measured accurately and an example
of the coordinated approach is in the development of the
X-ray thickness guage within the steel industry. As important as the coordinated investment is the agreement on standard formats of information to be collected so that information being collected by the Local Authority can be used on a
national basis. I would, therefore, recommend that the Department of Transport be used as the coordinating authority
both for the investment and production of a coordinated
specification. In making this decision it must be realized
that individual authorities must give way a little on their
personal requirements.

Mr S.J. Baker (Ferranti)

A systems approach is generally adopted in the automation of
plant. The objective is always to take input from the plant,
process this in some way at a central point and send outputs
to controls on the plant, which will then keep the product
within a product specification. This is a closed loop system
in the control engineering sense (not in the traffic engineering sense).

Such systems have been commercially available and in use since 1960. They have developed quite considerably since that time. One of the ways in which they have developed is that the central control office can be some distance away from the plant under control or the plant itself may be extremely extensive.

At an IEE conference on centralized computer control systems, an author working with a Water Authority described a data collection system for a river almost up to the source[4.1]. Here the data transmission involves not only cable lengths, but UHF radio as a spine, and VHF radio feeding into this spine. Similar techniques are used on systems for monitoring offshore oil pipelines and well heads, but here there is the added problem of getting all this data from the platforms to shore. This requires the use of further radio techniques in the troposcatter wavelengths.

I have used these examples to illustrate that systems approach, as used in automation, gives already extensive capability in data transmission and central computing.

Central computers have, for some time, been operating rapidly enough to take real-time inputs, process them and control a process. A traffic data collection system may not even be required to carry out processing. The point has already been made that such systems are not pressing the frontiers of technology.

What appears to be a shortcoming in the system approach to traffic data collection is a means whereby instrumentation is economically and readily connected to a central point for subsequent processing.

There is also a shortcoming on the clarification of the nature of the data which various users desire to extract from this data collection process. A systems approach to traffic data collection may help to identify these problems, perhaps to resolve many of them and to clarify the sorts of uncertainties that manufacturers have at the moment. This may lead to a stable market in which may be developed and sold products in which manufacturers are confident of the need.

Mr A. Roberts (BR Shipping Division)

The British Rail Shipping Division need data for revenue charging purposes, direct billing documentation, ship manifests, consignment notes, bills of lading and general management information.

We are interested in the possibilities stemming from an automated data collection system to speed the processing of vehicles through port checks. We are concerned with the

length of vehicles and the weight of commercial vehicles
from the point of view of ship's capacity. The linear and
volumetric capacity of the ship's deck is limited and we are
concerned with the weight from a deadweight point of view,
as ships must not be loaded below the Plimsol line.

The question of weight is becoming increasingly important
with the likelihood of increases from the present gross
vehicle weight maximum of 32 Imperial tons to possibly 40 or
44 metric tons.

There is a growing feeling in the Port and Shipping industry that in the near future, for environmental reasons, the
industry may be required to provide additional information
over that required at present.

Enquiries were made at The Department of Transport and TRRL
and in the trade about the possibility of automatic measuring
equipment. The indication received was that detector loop
systems would not give the degree of accuracy required.

Many optical systems, which were thought would give the
best solution were examined including film and TV. Lasers
were considered and eventually and infra-red system was
chosen. We became involved in developing a dynamic optical
modular electronic system for port use. The modular design
will allow for integration with other systems. The pattern
recognition could be by beam interruption or beam reflection.
We chose beam interruption. It will normally be a fixture
but it is transportable and can be operated by battery or
mains. It has been designed to complement a dynamic axle
weighing installation. Eventually it might be possible to
integrate such an installation so that the linear length
will be no more than 2½ m.

As indicated in Fig. 4.1, the vehicle passes through the
two measuring stations which are a fixed distance apart so
interrupting the two sets of beams. The system continuously
scans the vehicle as it passes through the light curtain,
and the resultant impulses are fed into a micro-processor to
calculate vehicle length. This model will incorporate an
automatic date/time stamp in the print-out of length, and
will also have an input keyboard facility, as the vehicle
registration number is needed for identification purposes.

The vehicles will initially be classified into one of
three categories, but there is the capability of making further analysis. In doing the calculations, there is an intermediate calculation which gives the mean speed of the vehicle,
and a spin-off is the potential to measure the distance
between axles to quite fine limits.

If the apparatus is cut down to about 3-ft. height above

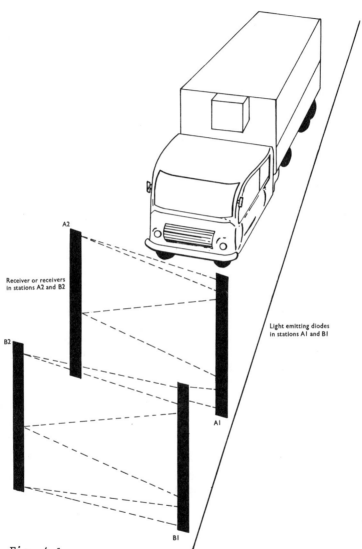

Receiver or receivers
in stations A2 and B2

Light emitting diodes
in stations Al and Bl

Fig. 4.1

the ground, using only one detector instead of the maximum
of three, this version would concentrate on the lower part
of a vehicle, and it would then have a use in connection
with axle weighing equipment for data collection and for
Traffic Law enforcement. It also has a possible interest and
application for monitoring the road-user aspect of unmanned
automatic level crossings where there are barriers of various sorts.

Sometimes it is only necessary to measure the trailer part
of an articulated unit. Fig. 4.2 illustrates that the top
beams are those needed to commence the measurement if only
the trailer is being shipped as an unaccompanied unit.

Mr P. Griffiths (Mangood Ltd)

The specification of systems and equipment requires discipline. The discipline of definition of requirement both of
technical need and installation time and the avoidance of
significant change.

As a manufacturer with a company who have designed and pro-
moted microprocessor based equipment for the past seven years,
I would say that microprocessors are a potential nightmare in
undisciplined hands.

The microprocessor is not the panacea of the indecisive
engineer. Significant changes to the specification of technical or operational requirements can be expensive and can
result in substantial delivery delays.

The user must be absolutely clear what his requirements
are because change is expensive and undesirable, the more so
when it is someone else's money.

The manufacturer has to have the benefit of foresight. He
has to anticipate need and, when offering a product whether
it is hardware or a system, he is offering the collective
experience of not one market but many.

I am not sure that I recognize the difference between the
specification and the code of practice. Whatever document is
issued it is meaningful and issued with good intent. Invariably it is changed. When dealing with data collection or
any other microprocessor based equipment it must be realized
that it is easy to change.

Mr Haldart (Ryksaterstaat, DP Division, Holland)

In Holland, there are two separate organizations, one is
governmental, more or less equivalent to the Department of
Transport and the other is the Provinces and is equivalent
to the counties in Britain. The provinces are totally auton-
omous, especially regarding budgets.

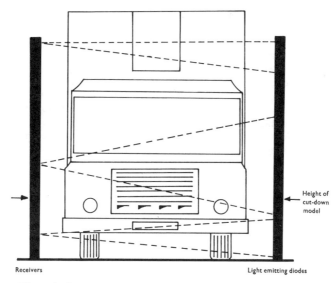

Fig. 4.2

The Dutch department of transport has about 170 permanent counting points where only the intensity of traffic is measured. There are about 500 periodic points of which 100 are sampled per annum. In five years all periodic points are covered. There are incidental points where measurements are done; there are about 50 for roads, bridges, junctions etc. Each province has about 40 permanent points and 50 periodic points. This is on the same basis as the department of transport but their capability of doing it automatically is limited because of their low funds.

The Dutch department of transport has much automated sampling material, but they do nearly all their counting automatically. In eleven provinces there are 500 permanent counting points and about 1000 periodic points which, even if they are only for intensities (for the department of transport they are sampled on an hourly basis; in the provinces they are half and half, hourly and daily) it makes for a lot of data.

For the last four years there has been co-operation between the government and the provinces, with the costs split between central and local government.

I am involved with data processing which is part of a department similar to the Department of the Environment in Britain. We have agreed with the provinces to make up data retrieval and storage systems for all traffic intensities.

The provinces do a lot of their sampling manually; they have not the funds to do it mechanically, so we have to find some basis on which we can do the normal use operations in a way in which all needs are covered.

It is an easy method of data handling but, since there are many types of counting, it is still àn important problem.

We hope to get the project right by about 1980. It is a similar situation to the British counties and government working together. It is a very expensive project and therefore one has to be very selective in what one needs. This is another advantage in working together.

Mr D.G. Clarke (Department of Transport)

Regardless of what some salesmen tell us, the cost of equipment and systems is approximately proportional to reliability and quality; one gets what one pays for. Pressure has reasonably been applied to keep the costs low, but this has resulted in the equipment price levels being too low to be taken seriously by industry.

The motorway communications system is not new. It is a fairly routine system and has been operating on our motorways for about 10 years, and the computing system controls 2,000 to 3,000 out stations. These out stations could equally well be data collection or census points. In serving these out stations, the system interrogates them regularly at five minute intervals, and collects information automatically. This information provides advice to the police and assists them in deciding what action to take. The information collected is automatically transmitted to the Department of Transport over the telephone network, where we are using it for operational purposes. This is not new, but a system of this kind could be used to meet some of the requirements raised at this conference. This reference serves only as an example to reinforce the point made by Mr Ham, that a system for the automatic collection of data is unlikely to pose serious technical problems.

I am in favour of a specification as opposed to codes of practice. Codes of practice issued in the past have not been taken as seriously as specifications. Consistency can be to everyone's long term advantage, but there is a price to pay; that is compliance by all users, including the Department. In my view specifications as opposed to codes of practice, issued on the systems and equipment for data collection would have a greater chance of achieving compliance.

Mr A.P. Goode (TRRL)

I am not yet convinced that we should be going all out for an automatic retrieval system. It has been within the state of the art for a number of years but has never come about. The point is that in order to get an automatic retrieval system, a great deal of thinking, man-power and design effort has to be invested. These systems break down through lack of those features. Is it likely that enough effort would be put into such a system to allow data to be collected effectively? There is great difficulty in maintaining good standards even in the very simple equipment used on the roads at present. I also have doubts about applying a code of practice or specification to data collection at this stage and I would put in a special plea for research here. Research can be restricted if one goes for codes of practice or specifications for equipment too early.

The conference has acknowledged the need to consider alternative methods in this field and research is continuing on this subject. The question of specification has to be approached warily so as not to inhibit people experimenting with new methods.

Mr D.G. Clarke (Department of Transport)

Commenting on Mr Goode's remarks regarding specifications being made too soon with the risk of inhibiting further research. There is always a risk, but within a development programme, one has to choose between awaiting for further development, and taking action. Our experience is that one should specify requirements when the market dictates the need for action, but to be prepared to amend the specifications as and when new developments emerge.

Mr C. Maxwell-Stewart (TPA)

As a consultant I have encountered situations where a so-called expert has advocated new technology for traffic counting systems and sounded like a genius in front of civil engineers, and yet appeared ridiculously out of date to electronic engineers.

I realise transport consultants are light years behind electronics experts. In trying to bring this expertise across the Atlantic one encounters a basic problem. There is a big difference between controlling and observing something like an inanimate object (eg a billet of red hot steel) and an object motivated by a human being; something which is essentially private. One immediately enters the political arena.

163

Another disincentive to using electronics is that labour is very cheap in the UK and there is a good supply of highly intelligent students and housewives who are prepared to work on surveys for about £1.50 an hour. In due course the cost of labour can be expected to rise in relation to the cost of electronic devices.

With increasingly stringent legislation, a move away from manual techniques has to be made, as relatively low standards of protection of the people who go out on the roads are accepted, and with more aggressive driving this will result in an increase in accidents.

It is very easy to maintain a piece of sophisticated equipment where one controls the environment. Traffic equipment which initially appeared very good has unfortunately fallen foul of the system with vandalism as one example. This is a real constraint on innovation.

Mr F.J. Gerachty (Department of Transport, TCC Division)

In TCC we are willing at any time to offer advice on service, care and maintenance of equipment. This service is also available from TRRL. This is of course within the limits of the resources available to us, but sometimes if enough pressure is brought to bear the resources can be made available.

If care is taken on installation of road sensors, the suppliers of the equipment counting packages are fully aware of the very hostile environment in which they have to operate. They are constantly looking for means to improve this and to keep costs down.

Our very simple data retrieval system uses the Post Office public telephone subscriber network. The accuracy achieved from manual versus the automatic count is an error rate of 0.3% for 30,000 vehicles. This illustrates just how capable the automatic counting equipment is.

On the costs of implementing the system postulated by Mr Ham, all the capital costs do not need to be incurred at the same time. Road sensors can be laid down and used without having got as far as providing all the sophistication of data retrieval and the ordinary counters can be provided.

When one is ready to implement sophisticated field stations, the same loop and sensor array and the same cabinet housing on the side of the road can be used.

We the engineers and technologists can offer equipment and facilities which will enable the necessary data to be obtained at a reasonable price and in a reasonable period of time.

Mr B. Stagg (West Midlands)

The Department of Transport seems to want to move away from manual data collection, but from the local authority point of view, there are always surveys which have to be done manually. As an example, the seat belt survey is one which I do not think will ever be automated. To retain manual counts, advances in technology in that direction must be sought.

One of the problems of manual data collection is that there is a stage beyond that of transcription before the data is put into the computer.

If the technological steps can be taken, not only in automatic collection but also manual collection, we will be moving further forward than by simply sticking to the automatic side of data collection. It would be equally valuable if the County Surveyors society could also look at the manual side of data collection.

The Chairman

I am very conscious of what I call the TCC do-it-yourself world which has tended to limit skills in this field. An attempt has been made to interest the private sector so that their existing skill may be extended to the benefit of export. I would be interested to see what the association of consulting engineers have to say about their interests and the need for these skills in overseas markets.

Mr G. Bingham (G. Maunsell and Partners)

The consulting engineers in this field are very much in a similar position to many local authorities. They usually have a specific local problem to deal with. Usually there will be some data collection necessary which the consulting engineer will have to undertake himself, it may be by mechanical or manual means. I believe that the more we can do mechanically, the better it will be for us in the long run, but I do not believe we shall ever completely eliminate manual surveying.

With almost every study one gets, there is a vast amount of background data which has to be collected, usually from at least two county authorities, various local authorities and, almost invariably, from the Department. The amount of work and time that can be wasted in integrating all these different collections of data can be phenomenal. The more that the Department can do to develop a degree of standardization in the background data, on which we all have to fall back in the end, will be enormously helpful and a great sav-

165

ing in the amount of work to be done in future studies.
Studies cost too much these days.

Mr J.B. Evans (Halcrow Fox and Associates)

I am surprised that cost benefit has not been mentioned in
this conference. Anyone can express an opinion that a technique is worthwhile but in quoting figures such as 0.3%
accuracy surely one also has to demonstrate that one has
achieved something worthwhile.

The ultimate in technology is not always the base. Humbler
(intermediate) technology can often prove better in the long
run, especially when questions of maintenance and reliability
are taken into account.

Mr G. Jones (Wootton, Jeffreys and Partners)

My firm offers transportation planning and computer consult-
ancy using mini and micro computers on a bureau basis. I
see a potential for a consultant which is not that of the
traditional consultant service. The type of equipment discussed at the conference involves costs of some tens of thou-
sands of pounds. With this expenditure the equipment must
be used effectively.

Authorities, in general, will not be able to afford this
expenditure, and are unlikely to be able to use it continuously. There is a potential for the hiring of the equipment for specific uses, together with the computer analysis
and the expertise in surveying and interpretation, similar
to that provided by specialist computer bureaux. Who should
provide this? The manufacturers probably do not want to, as
their job is to manufacture and to create new designs. We
suggest this is a role the consultants should fulfil and
accordingly are investing in the equipment and the development of analysis packages, to blend our micro computer experience to our knowledge of the transportation area.

Dr J.G.M. Wood (Flint and Neill, Consulting Engineers)

The prospect of instant data retrieval on vehicle flows is
tempting. While it is essential for traffic control it is
undesirable and unnecessary for traffic data for analysis.

For analysis it is essential to have the data stored in a
compact and readily accessible form. The data starts as
pulses from detectors which can either be stored on tape or
partially analysed and condensed before storage. For this
pre-analysis and condensation a clear and standard definition of terminology is essential. How this is specified is

less important than that it is on a consistent and standard-
ized basis. For example it must be clear whether vehicle
length is the distance between the first and last axle, or
from bumper to bumper, and how vehicle spacing is calculated.
The errors in classification likely must also be made clear
e.g. between light goods and cars.

The greater the amount of pre-analysis the less data needs
to be stored, but the picture of the traffic obtained will
be blurred. There is therefore a strong case for keeping a
limited sample of highly detailed vehicle by vehicle records
such as those described in Paper 9. The rest of the data
can then be condensed.

Finally it is essential to remember that computers can't
read print and that all data for subsequent analysis must be
kept on tape. Piles of printout are useless.

Mr P. Rix (Devon County Council)

The counties and also the Department of Transport must recognize the danger of collecting so much data that much remains
unused. Returning to data to find it in its original state
two or three years later is rarely done because it is both
inconvenient and is unlikely to be suitable because of
changes in events.

The way ahead is possibly to summarize data very carefully
immediately after collection and use the summaries to answer
the everyday traffic questions that are asked. Microfilming
and magnetic tape can then be used to store the raw data if
such storage is required, provided access to the data in
this form is convenient. It is at the summary stage that
presentation of data is of the utmost importance - and I consider a graphical approach to be the best.

With regard to the question of automatic counter hire - in
Devon there are about 80 automatic counters to cover 8000
miles of road with a back up supply of 20 older automatic
counters which are used for specific surveys in the summer.
There are times in August, however, when it would be useful
to have more as back up counters to a day's classified count
for example, and it would be advantageous to hire equipment
in these circumstances.

From Devon's point of view a non-random sampling technique
is required to ensure a good traffic counter coverage of the
road network. I emphasize non-random as opposed to the Department's random choice of sites used for the 200 point surveys. I believe that a non-random choice of site should use a
technique based on road characteristic (identified by the
annual, weekly, and daily profiles of a traffic counter at a
particular site) and not by using road class as is the current
practice.

Discussion on Papers 9 and 10

The Chairman

Why do you necessarily feel you need to use all the data you
collect? It may be sufficient to recognize the differences
and throw away the data if nothing has changed.

Mr P. Rix (Devon County Council)

We collect data for many reasons. The counties have specific
reasons which they know about in advance and because it is
an expensive process to collect it, analyse it and edit it,
we are anxious to use all the data collected.

The Chairman

Not as expensive as the uncertainties which may arise from
not having data, where you recognize differences are occurring.

Mr Rix

Some of these changes can be observed by referring to permanent counter sites if they are sited with care.

D. Fryer (Department of the Environment and Transport)

Careful stock of the present situation should be taken before
embarking upon the new methods of automatic data collection.
It is less easy to argue the case for a costly national network of automatic traffic counters than it might have been in
the mid-sixties when, though traffic growth was phenomenal,
counts, modest in both scale and means sufficed. If today's
needs are sensibly different they should be closely defined
before any attempt is made to satisfy them, and only then if
it can be shown beyond doubt that the ends justify the means.
Given that axle loadings are critically important as the key
determinant in carriageway longevity, it scarcely follows
that automatic sensors should be employed on a mammoth scale
to measure their magnitude and the frequency of their occurrence when in the majority of cases they might have been arrived at by other means. In this connection an acceptable
level of accuracy still needs to be declared. In any event
- and this applies equally to speed, headway and lane changing propensity (those three important behavioural responses
to level of flow) - it is arguably better to consider the
phenomenon on a strictly ad hoc basis, when economies may
be looked for in terms of both scale and method.
    The greatest effort should be directed to vehicle classif-
ication, the most important of these data categories.
    Existing census methods should be examined to see if they

could be advantageously modified, before decisions are made
as to the extent of the introduction of automatic classification.

The General Traffic Census, expensive, unwieldy, monolithic
and, above all, non-specific, yields data having either a
gratuitous value or none at all. It might well be the case
that unwittingly, by making GTC inflexible, the Department
of Transport has provided not only local authorities, but
also its own regional organisations with the incentive to
initiate counting programmes of their own, the scale of which
has so much diminished the always tenuous value of GTC as to
suggest its immediate discontinuance. To abandon GTC and at
the same time, by common consent and co-operation, to structure and co-ordinate the census activities of local authorities and regional offices could only be worthwhile. Admitt-
edly data flow would in the main assume the form of unclassified time-referenced totals, but, for the most part, this
is all that is required, since local need (and local need is
paramount) has traditionally been well served by occasional
calibration counts. Superfluous counting should certainly
be discouraged, and in this connection it should be acknowledged that continuous automatic counting does indeed produce
a plethora of data. Two points deserve to be considered, the
first concerning itself with the need to count continuously
at all, and the second with the need to count in small increments of time throughout the counting period. In many situations periodic counting is enough: in others it would be
worthwhile having hourly suppression switches fitted to the
counters to permit small-increment counting during specified
periods and 16- and 24-hour summations only at all other
times. This would stem the flow of unwanted data and go a
long way to making data processing a less daunting task.
Data should continue to be retrieved by agent authorities who
are both accustomed and well-suited to perform the task.

The 200-Point Census on which classified vehicle-kilometres
and related accident rates so much depend must be treated
with the utmost circumspection. Even here, however, some
economies may be attainable through the complementary use of
automatic counters at every census point. It seems likely
that the unclassified output of these counters could be calibrated satisfactorily via existing periodic manual counts
which, themselves, could be reduced in frequency wherever
historic records showed volumetric fluctuations to be matched
proportionately throughout the classification range.

Good housekeeping requires that we make the most of all
the data collection resources at our command before embarking
on a programme of expansion. The first priority should be
to utilize more fully the considerable but diffuse data that

Discussion on Papers 9 and 10

is simply lying around unused.

The Chairman

The Traffic engineering Division of the Department of Transport have put out a note on the management of data collection which is required reading for anyone involved.[4.2]

REFERENCES

4.1 Hanson, C.A. and Cameron, A.M. (1978). Evolution of computer based river management systems. *2nd. Int. Conf. Centralized Computer Control Systems*. IEE Conference Publication 161.

4.2 A manual of practice on automatic traffic counting. Draft for comment and interim guidance. TE/240/7, Sept. 1977, Traffic Engineering Division, Department of Transport.

Summing-up

Mr R.J. Bridle, BSc and Mr R.E. Fry, BSc MIS
Department of Transport

The conference produced a most valuable perspective on the problems which still face us in the field of traffic data collection. The range of those problems has clearly given rise to a variety of views among those active in the field, on the possibilities for progress. Some were pessimistic (or at least cautious) while others claimed, on the basis of experience, that many of those problems could be overcome now. On balance, this exchange of views favoured the optimists and gave a number of pointers to the way forward.

To take the technical and operational problems first, there was a general view that we must improve the accuracy of traffic flow data, solve the problems of data management, and extend the range of information collected to include the parameters of speed, headway between vehicles and axle loads. All of this points firmly in the direction of greater use of automatic equipment. There is by now widespread experience in both central and local government in the use of certain types of automatic equipment. However this experience has not all been favourable and has brought new problems in its wake.

Most notably, there have been difficulties in maintaining the sensors installed on the road surface. Pneumatic tubes are rapidly damaged by heavy traffic and will ultimately produce incorrect signals and eventually cease to operate altogether. Since continuity and accuracy of data are the virtues particularly sought from automatic equipment, this is a considerable disadvantage. Inductive loops are more secure from traffic-inflicted damage but in urban areas may be accidentally dug up by various public service undertakings, with uncomfortable frequency. Moreover the greater expense and difficulty of their installation militates against that mobility of location which is sometimes required.

Summing-up

Even when operating normally, continuous sensors are likely to register nontypical data due to unforeseen events (accidents, parked vehicles, temporary traffic management schemes) which if not correlated with the data can produce misleading information.

Problems with the on-site counters are rather less prominent although local authorities have had maintenance problems with some electro-mechanical types. However there is a lack of clarity here about the range of technical possibilities which are or might become available); and uncertainty about the direction in which development should be encouraged. Doubts were expressed about the ability of industry to produce suitable equipment on a sufficient scale and within a reasonable period.

A factor which inhibited some authorities from going too far in the direction of automatic recording was the question of how one should manage, store and effectively use the very large volumes of data which would be generated by large-scale automation - a problem enhanced by the discontinuities and corruption in the data now being experienced.

Reassurance on most of these points was offered by those (mainly the Department of Transport, TRRL, some local authorities and private sector firms) who already had successful experience in running and maintaining fairly large automated systems. Many of the problems with automatic counters arose from the lack of operational back-up. For example, the TRRL experience in running the 50-point automated traffic census had shown the need, even with simple equipment, for regular on-site checking and maintenance work carried out to specified standards by specially trained field teams. New and promising tribo-electric forms of axle detector were already undergoing extensive testing and might in time replace pneumatic tubes. Many problems of reliability could be considerably reduced by setting higher standards of on-site installation and by providing proper workshop facilities either at base or in mobile form.

Industry representatives responded to doubts about their ability to deliver the goods by making the point that a necessary prerequisite was for the public sector to achieve a consensus view on desirable directions of development and to plan for installation on a scale which would make greater investment in development and production facilities, worthwhile. At the same time they pointed to the comparatively wide range of technical options already in existance and displayed in the exhibition accompanying the conference.

Perhaps the most important challenges remaining were in the fields of data format, storage, editing, and analysis.

172

The point was made that the fact that continuous monitoring
potentially produced very large volumes of data was not
necessarily a serious problem. There was for example no
need for the retention of indefinite quantities of historic
data, except on a highly selective basis for a specific purpose. Undoubtedly, full exploitation of the information on
the detailed patterns of traffic flow (the key feature of
continuous monitoring) called for advanced methods of data
processing.

There was no lack of interesting possibilities here, but
some of these implied systems of some complexity. Past
experience of over-ambitious computerized systems indicated
the need for caution, a high level of expertise and a clear
link between output and usage. The need for development in
this area would be reinforced by the more widespread use of
equipment like that developed by TRRL which through special
sensor arrays linked to an on-site programmable microprocessor could produce not only traffic flows, but vehicle
classifications, speeds and headways.

Both the Department of Transport and senior local
authority representatives deduced from all this the need for
much greater coordination of ideas and activities. The
Department should take a broad view of the national (as
opposed to Departmental) needs for traffic information and
give a lead in technical development in the areas of equipment and data management. The germs of this approach were
contained in the outline proposals for the reform of the
Departmental traffic censuses in the opening paper of the
conference by Mr Fry.

On a wider front, the Chairman drew attention to the fact
that the conference had (as originally intended) devoted
itself solely to currently observed technical problems in
traffic data collection. Those problems were urgent and
deserved attention now - and yet there was a sense in which
they could never be finally resolved until we had given
thought to a more fundamental problem. That was the question as to whether the data and its uses were best suited to
meet the requirements of transportation policy and management.

It could not be assumed that our procedures for using the
data to inform policy and management decisions were either
definitive or optimum. In the course of discussion, some
speakers had in fact drawn attention to aspects of this situation in the field of highway scheme design and appraisal.
Thus, some of the concepts used were lacking in rigour and
precision. Again, there were disturbing gaps such as the
lack of factors for the estimation of design parameters

which were specific to local schemes.

In areas of civil engineering practice, it is usual to distinguish between specifications and codes of practice. Specifications are concerned with standards for materials and systems, while codes of practice are concerned with proper usage of those systems. As compared with some longer established areas (as for example bridge engineering) traffic engineering noticeably lacks thoroughly worked-out standards of either kind. This conference had given useful guidance on how we might move towards agreed specifications. There is perhaps a serious case for a further conference on codes of practice. There is very considerable scope for detailed study in this area which would have a small price in relation to the quantum leap that might result in traffic engineering practice.

The Chairman suggested that there might be some connection between this aspect and the fact that the conference discussion produced no serious critique of the Departmental proposals for reform of its own traffic censuses. And yet in one important sense they were strongly ratified. This was where they made the case for a common traffic data format and data organisation as between central and local government. Achievement of that was strongly linked with the ideal of a rigorously based common glossary and common set of procedures for the profession as a whole. Not the least of the benefits for local and central government that might emerge from that would be the presentation of compatible views at public inquiries into highway schemes.